# ALL YOU LOVE IS NEED

THIRD · WAY · BOOKS

# ALL YOU LOVE IS NEED

### Tony Walter

First published in Great Britain 1985
SPCK
Holy Trinity Church
Marylebone Road
London NW1 4DU

*Extracts from the article 'Shere Hite on Maleness
and Mixed Feelings' are reproduced by
permission of* Spare Rib.

*The Collect of Purity from The Order for
Holy Communion Rite A in The Alternative
Service Book 1980 is reproduced with
permission.*

*British Library Cataloguing in Publication Data*

Walter, J. A.
   All you love is need. — (Third way books)
   1. Sociology
   I. Title      II. Society for Promoting
   Christian Knowledge      III. Series
   301      HM51

   ISBN 0-281-04178-4

Filmset by Pioneer, East Sussex
Printed in Great Britain by
Whitstable Litho Ltd, Whitstable, Kent

*To the memory of
a true colleague,
Godfrey Williams.*

# Contents

# THIRD WAY BOOKS
## Series Editor: Tim Dean

*Third Way Books* aim to explore the relation between biblical Christian faith and political, social and cultural life. SPCK and *Third Way* magazine have joined together to publish a series that will introduce some contemporary writing to a wide audience.

*Third Way* is an evangelical magazine which seeks to provide a biblical perspective on politics, social ethics and cultural affairs. Further details from: *Third Way*, 37 Elm Road, New Malden, Surrey KT3 3HB.

# Acknowledgements

I cannot hope to list all those who have helped me think through the subject of need, but I would like especially to thank the following: Peter Schouls, Diana Burfield, Keith White, Phil and Miriam Sampson, Sally Macintyre, Shirley Garner, Graham Room and David Perkins for commenting on particular chapters; June Osborne, Pat Ryan, and some members of the Ilkley Study Group for discussing an early draft of chapter 6; Annette Holman, Richard and Janice Russell, Joan Oldman and Godfrey Williams for patiently listening and responding at various stages. Jill Jones typed cheerfully and competently. Finally, thank you to Tim Dean, and the publishers and their advisers, for help in editing a text that proved stubborn in places.

# Preface

Laments about materialism are rife, denouncing our need for material things. But belief that certain things are necessary and indispensable is much more widespread than even the most ardent lamenters of materialism suppose. Many men, for example, seem to need paid employment in order to be men, and increasingly women are coming to feel a similar need. Many women need to bear a child in order to be complete women. Many people of both sexes think that life will be less than complete without a mate. It is fashionable to follow the view of some psychologists that the self is a bundle of needs and that personal growth is the business of progressively meeting these needs. Many Christians go along with such beliefs.

But is this just tagging along with the spirit of the age? The Christian faith is founded on a man whom Christians believe to be the most complete person this world has ever known. By present standards, this man was poor in material things. He was not married, had no children, and gave up his job in order to become an itinerant and unpaid preacher. The totalitarian Roman Empire in which he lived denied him many of those things which today are regarded as basic human needs. Moreover Jesus taught that, far from basing our life on the needs of the self, we should take up our cross and deny our self. Yet nobody, least of all those who knew him, has ever called Jesus an ascetic. Some of them even criticized him for enjoying life.

This picture of Jesus suggests that work, parenthood, marriage, sex, human company, material goods, and all the good things of life are precisely that: the good things of life. But we do not *need* them in order to become complete persons, to be human. They can never become the basis for a fulfilled existence. They are, literally, *goods* (not commodities, but things good in themselves). In a world richly endowed by God, there are too many good things for us to be dependent on any one for a full life.

This is in complete contrast to what most people believe today. They say, 'Well, if people didn't need to work, then nobody would work. If people didn't need company, then they'd become hermits.' The only basis for work, or any human activity, they can conceive of is need. Marriage is seen as a contract in which I meet your needs in return for your meeting my needs; 'I love you' now means 'I need you'. Child rearing and education are fashionably seen as a matter of meeting children's needs, rather than teaching them knowledge or values. Even holidays and sports are seen as meeting leisure needs and recreational needs created by the pressures and unhealthiness of factory, office or kitchen. Is this really the free, fun-loving society we suppose ours to be? So many of the things that Jesus saw as *goods,* people today can conceive of only as a meeting of a need, an escape from a *bad.*

What alternative is there? While pointing sadly to the fact that people do indeed act out of weakness and need, the biblical writers along with other sages through human history held a vision of an alternative way of life. Not struggling through work, marriage or a programme of self-actualization to create a self out of nothing, but responding to the pre-existing love and grace found both in God and in the groups to which we all belong. This involves rejecting the achievement-oriented individualism of our time and rediscovering the freedom found in community. And there are many implications for personal living, for welfare arrangements, and for society.

Liberation theology has so far focused on how those in the Third World can liberate themselves from their visible oppression. It has failed to show how Christianity promises freedom in modern Western societies, because it has not understood the nature of oppression in such societies, which is often internal as much as external. It is the voice of new inner needs, not the whip of the plantation owner, that enslaves us. People believe that affluence enables them to graduate from consumption of necessities to consumption of luxuries, that history is now liberating them from the necessities of work to the freedom of leisure, that personal growth involves a graduation from basic needs (security, love, etc.) to free self-fulfilment. But these are all lies. The evidence consistently shows *new* needs to be created by these very processes of affluence, personal growth and history. *This* is the peculiarly modern prison for which, if we really mean business by liberation, we must find a key.

Part One documents need in selected areas. Part Two reviews and assesses this. If there is one chapter which contains the nub of the book, then it is chapter 10, 'Needs Must'; the reader whose approach to books is one of dipping rather than ploughing should ensure he does not miss that chapter. As it is not the easiest chapter, however, it should perhaps not be the first dip!

# INTRODUCTION

# 1: A New Morality

A new morality is all about us, and virtually nobody has noticed. Its centrepiece is 'need'. Needs are good things, and meeting need is the ultimate good.

Of course, everybody knows that morals are changing. There may be some dispute as to how much people's behaviour is changing, but there is no disagreement that the grounds of moral appeal are changing. How may I justify my behaviour, to myself and to others? What were once acceptable as good reasons, such as 'God says . . .', 'The Bible says . . .', 'The Church says . . .', 'My parents always taught me so', 'I ought', 'You have a duty to', are rarely heard today, and sound old-fashioned.

What reasons *are* supposed to be acceptable today? Humanism and democracy both elevate the reason and the will of the individual; 'I choose', 'I want' and 'I have decided' are now perfectly respectable justifications for behaviour, with the sole proviso that my choice does not harm others. This is the 'new morality' which so shocked traditionalists in the 1960s.

Many who are unhappy with current moral changes would concur that there is more choice available today; they complain that youngsters especially 'have far too much freedom to do as they please nowadays'. They may disagree with humanists as to the desirability of personal freedom to do as one pleases, but they agree that 'I want' is becoming a popular motive. Some religious language too reflects the change and makes central the individual's choice. Whereas once the new convert saw himself as responding to the moral demands of God, now he sees himself as having made a personal decision to follow Jesus. 'Thou shalt' is replaced by 'I choose'.

Some philosophers in the last century considered human happiness to be our main purpose in life. If something made people happy, then it was by definition a good thing. Maximizing pleasure and minimizing pain were deemed good motives. And it would seem that they may have succeeded in replacing traditional morality by the language of happiness and pleasure, if one is to believe those vociferous guardians of the old order, from Malcolm Muggeridge in Britain to the Moral Majority in the States, who castigate our age for its hedonism. Personal pleasure and fun are what people live for now, they complain. Certainly 'It's fun' is a justification that is hard to argue against.

The opinion of most commentators on modern life is that the traditional moral language of 'I ought' has been replaced by the language of 'I want', 'I choose', and 'It's fun'. Each person is now out for himself.

That's what the pundits think. But are they right? If you actually listen to the language of people in everyday life (and this includes the language of the pundits themselves when they are not pontificating on what motivates others), you will hear remarkably little about choices, pleasures and wants. Actions which are manifestly not prescribed by biology or society and which are the choice of the individual are talked of more often than not as necessities rather than as choices. We are more likely to hear 'The car needs washing' than 'I've decided to wash the car'. The television advertisement is as likely to say 'You need Vim' as 'Next time, why not choose Vim?'

Probably the housewife has more scope to organize her working day and the nature of her tasks than most other workers. Yet housework which *she* has devised to meet the standards of cleanliness *she* has decided on are experienced as one 'must' after another: 'The dishes need doing', 'Jim's trousers need mending', 'I must get the washing out before it rains'. This occupation involves more people than any other. It provides vast scope for personal organization of the work by the worker, and yet the language of choice is hardly ever heard. It seems as though the houseworker imprisons herself by continually experiencing personally decided-upon courses of action as necessities.[1]

If anything is motivated by free will, surely it is love. Love that is not freely given is not love. Yet even in love and marriage, the language of need is taking over. 'I love you, darling' has become 'I need you, baby'. Marriage today is not the mutual giving of self, but the mutual meeting of each partner's needs by the other; if one partner's needs are no longer being met by the other, then this is widely deemed as grounds for divorce. 'I could no longer meet his/her needs'; he/she could no longer meet my needs' is the cry of the partner who walks out, and this is accepted in many circles. It is not a matter of choice, but of necessity.

That other major form of love, charity, is also reconceived in terms of needs. Personal philanthropy that reached out to the sick and suffering has been replaced by bureaucratized welfare in which the person is conceived as a bundle of needs; the system splits this bundle into several parts and allocates each to the particular profession (medicine, social work, chiropody, or whatever) that is in business to meet that need. Charity, the total giving of one person to the totality of another, is out of fashion, and is hardly possible in a welfare system dominated by bureaucracy and professionalism.

Even holidays and vacations, though they clearly have little other purpose, are rarely justified in terms of pleasure and fun. 'I/you need a break,' we say. Many people frown on taking a vacation until they need it. Planners, politicians and social scientists talk of the 'recreational needs' of the masses. The popular press, magistrates and social workers frown with disapproval when some youngster, out for a good time on a Saturday night which gets him into trouble of some kind, simply says in his defence, 'It was fun', or, 'I did it for kicks'.

If we are such a fun-loving, hedonistic society of self-determining individuals, why do we hear so little of pleasure and choice in everyday talk? Why so much appeal to need and necessity? Most of us, most of the time, do not experience ourselves as masters of our own destiny, freely choosing our own pleasures. No, we feel ourselves to be slaves to necessity. The best reason that I can give for an action is that I, or you, need it. This is the new morality. This is the new language that tells you and me whether or not what I am doing is right.

There is a popular misconception, especially among those who read too much philosophy and listen too little to their next door neighbours or even to themselves, that science demonstrates how all our actions are pre-programmed or determined by biology, genes, environment, upbringing and so on, and that the sense of free will and of being able to choose is an illusion.

I suspect the evidence points to precisely the opposite.

Science shows us how unprogrammed human beings are, compared to other species. Most species are largely governed by instinct and have no choice. The vast majority of human behaviour, however, is learnt, which means that we learn how to act by adopting the cultural rules of our particular society. And there is no evidence that the diversity of human cultures is programmed in detail by biology; my genes do not tell me to use a knife and fork any more than the Chinaman's tell him to use chopsticks. But while we actually are free, we *feel* we have no choice. I *need* my knife and fork. I need my laundry powder, and the knowledge that most of humanity has got along without laundry powder and knives and forks in no way reduces my need. In precisely those areas where biology leaves us free, society steps in and takes away that freedom. Natural science shows us to be remarkably free; it is in everyday life that we imprison ourselves by creating needs for ourselves. We put ourselves in need.

To say we are *slaves* to necessity, however, does not capture the whole of people's experience of themselves as in need, for on the whole we actually welcome our needs. Everyone agrees it is good that we should have needs, and even better that those needs should be met; and it is this that makes the contemporary language of need a *moral* language.

People today assume that needs are not bad things to be eliminated, but good things to be met. The pop singer crooning 'I need you baby' is positively rejoicing in his state of need. More seriously, we spend our lives exploring this rich world, not joyfully but out of weakness, to solve some inner need. We get married because we cannot bear the prospect of life alone; we have children in response to what we conceive as maternal, or paternal, need; we go to the countryside because we need fresh air and a dose of wild nature; our work is dominated by psychological needs for security and recognition. And all of this is seen as a good thing. A society in which people are not motivated by need simply would not be possible, we think — for people would not have children if they did not need to, and so on. Needs are conceived of as good things without which society could not operate. (This view is thoroughly ingrained in psychiatry, psychology, sociology and economics.) We actually want to be in need.

This has not always been so. In the Stoic and Christian traditions, for example, a person's needs and desires were often believed to be at war with the moral demands of God or the good of society. More recently, Sigmund Freud believed that there are fundamental conflicts between the biological needs and desires of the unconscious id and the conscience of the superego, between self and society, between 'I need' and 'I ought', conflicts that are resolved by the 'I will' of the ego. But Freud's psychology is replaced now in the popular bookstores and on many psychiatric couches by the humanistic psychology of writers such as Fromm, Maslow and Rogers, whose ideal personality is one in which the needs of the individual can be, should be or are met by society. The personality is a bundle of needs, life's project is the progressive meeting of them, and society is the midwife of this gradual emergence of the 'self-actualized person'.

One mark of the almost total success of this new morality is that the Christian Church, traditionally keen on mortifying the desires of the flesh, on crucifying the needs of the self in pursuit of the religious life, has eagerly adopted the language of needs for itself. To the long queues of doctors, salesmen, advertisers and pop-song lovers peddling their wares with the slogan that they will meet our needs, we now hear that 'Jesus will meet your every need', as though he were some kind of divine psychiatrist or divine detergent, as though God were there simply to service us. Enthusiastic young Christians hopefully implore God to meet their various wants and needs, whereas the medieval ascetic would have prayed for strength to deny his needs. Then, when some of his needs are *not* met by Jesus — as the medievals knew full well they would not be — the modern convert is liable to abandon his faith with as much just cause for complaint as the person who leaves his marriage partner for the same reason: that the expectation of total need satisfaction has not been fulfilled. Likewise, social gospel churches see their job as meeting the needs of the local community as though God were some kind of ultimate welfare agency.

Is this new escalation of needs just a new way of talking about our wants? Do we say 'I need' when we know perfectly well that what we really mean is 'I want'? Is it just a linguistic cover-up for rampant hedonism?

Well, sometimes people do say 'I need' in this way, but by no means always. Need is far more subtle, and consequently more powerful, than that. Often wants and needs are directly in conflict. The hospital patient who says, 'I feel better now, doctor, I want to go home,' may be confronted with the reply, 'You're still very weak. You need to stay here.' Possibly the main issue in the philosophy of welfare today is whether services should be provided to meet the conscious wants of clients (the consumer model of welfare) or to meet the clients' needs as determined authoritatively by the professional worker (the paternalist model of welfare). Inherent in the practice of social work is the distinction between the presenting problem (what the client says he wants, what he says is his problem) and what the social worker assesses is the real underlying need. My 'I want' is likely to be overridden, rightly or wrongly, by some professional saying, 'Maybe, but you need something else'. Certainly all children quickly learn that what they want is often overridden by what their parents say they need.

Also, if 'I need' means no more than 'I want', then people would not experience what they call needs as needs. They would know that it's just a way of talking. Sometimes it is. But when a housewife goes to the supermarket saying she needs some more laundry powder, she really means she needs it, not just wants it, and won't be able to do the washing without it. When an unemployed woman says she needs a job, she means it. When a man says he needs his wife and would be lost without her, he doesn't just mean he loves her, likes her or desires her, but that he really does need her.

Need really is what motivates people much of the time. Of course, there are many times when it is also used as a convenient rationalization after the event, covering up a whole range of other motives. But that is typical of any morality. Any morality both deeply motivates people and provides convenient rationalizations. Duty to family or country, for example, have in the past been the wellspring of many actions, and at the same time have provided a convenient excuse for not considering the effects of one's actions on others less closely related than family or fellow countrymen. It is precisely because a moral code provides a general language for talking about behaviour that, in any society, rationalizations are usually given in the language of the dominant moral code; any other language would be less credible. So my argument that need has become a new moral language does not hinge on whether or not, or how often, people use this language with less than total conviction. The language of the Ten Commandments did not have to motivate even one tenth of the actions of middle-class Victorian society for it to be the moral language of that society.[2]

In fact, if people do say 'need' when they mean 'want', this is very strong evidence for my argument. If our society really values choice and freedom and pleasure, why don't people say 'I want' when they mean 'I want'? Why is it more respectable, easier, more persuasive, to say 'I need'? Surely because need is known to be accepted as a more legitimate motive, a morally better motive.

## Needs and Progress

Needs, and talk of needs, are certainly proliferating. The catalogue of my local library lists books by the score with *need* in the title: modern needs, the needs of adolescents, the needs of ex-prisoners, the training needs of new foremen, the long-term irrigation needs for England and Wales, basic human needs, common human needs, special educational needs, the needs of children, the needs of industry, sexual needs, emotional needs, housing needs, family needs, community needs, organizational necessities and individual needs, manpower needs, energy needs, the needs of single people, the needs of homeless people, research needs, social needs. And that's only a start. The list seems endless. Virtually every aspect of human existence is now talked of as a need.

Many, if not most, of these needs are new. And certainly talking of them as needs is new. A person's need for paid employment certainly did not exist in the largely non-money economies of medieval villages or of tribal societies. The need for laundry powder is rather new. Many of the emotional needs which spouses meet in each other may have been created by the pressures of our consumerist, industrial, urban society. Is this proliferation of needs a good thing?

Clearly the manufacturers of the goods that meet the new needs think so. Also psychologists think it a mark of personal progress that the individual can advance from being concerned with basic needs like food or security to more advanced emotional needs. And even Karl Marx thought that to be a man of few needs was the mark of the primitive, and he looked forward to a society and to a personality rich in needs. All these believers in human progress believe the history of civilization to be the progressive meeting of our simpler needs, so allowing more complex and rewarding needs to emerge. Creating and meeting need is what makes the world go round. Marx and Engels spoke for them all when they said that, 'the satisfaction of the first need leads to new needs; and this production of new needs is the first historical act'.[3] Never did the nineteenth-century voice of progress speak more clearly.

An alternative interpretation of the proliferation of needs finds it a strange kind of progress that can conceive of the richness of human life only as a series of necessities, and that re-writes history to say that this has ever been so. Factually, it is hardly correct to say that people have always been pre-occupied with their needs. There is widespread evidence that 'unsophisticated' tribes are usually very concerned with religion and ritual, with community and family life; for these are what enable them to make sense of what appear to us as prior states of need such as hunger and sickness.

The biblical writers believed that creation was richly endowed by God and that life was full of blessings — good health, fertility, national security — which were to be enjoyed and appreciated when available, but which did not destroy the meaning of life when removed (though people have always found this hard to accept, as many of the more despairing Psalms demonstrate). These writers portrayed the good things of life as blessings, not needs; not, as the dictionary puts it, 'things which one cannot well do without'. The focus was on the Giver, not the receiver.

When human beings believe themselves to be self-sufficient, however, as has become fashionable over the last couple of hundred years, then human needs take centre stage. Alone in the universe, what else can we put at the centre? I sometimes feel that perhaps we cannot actually cope with the very real choices and freedoms offered by modern society and by its view of human beings as autonomous, that we cannot bear the personal responsibility of choosing, and so we welcome the creation of new needs, material or psychological, by which our lives can be directed. With nothing outside of ourselves to live for which could direct our choices, we make our own needs the focus of our lives, and this results in the negation of choice. We experience manifestly good things, such as creativity in our work or the joy of romantic love, and elevate them into idols which we cannot do without.[4]

Every political party, religion or social movement today offers liberation. They usually offer liberation from external constraints: socialism and feminism have a vision in which people are no longer dominated economically and politically by others. Liberation theology constantly refers to South America, where the domination of the poor is particularly concrete and visible. One reason, perhaps, that socialism fails to gain much support among the better-off members of the better-off nations is that such people have had many of their obvious shackles removed. The proletariat of the nineteenth century has been replaced by the affluent working class of the mid-twentieth century, and the labour movement struggles to find supporters; the old appeal to workers to throw off their shackles makes little sense when the shackles are no longer very obvious. Liberation theology may look fine in South America, or to North American blacks, but white Christians in western Europe and North America have considerable difficulty in applying it to their own lives.

One response is to show how we have internalized many of our constraints. The women's movement, for example, shows not only how women are barred by a male-dominated system from economic and political equality, but also how women limit themselves by their belief in the inevitability of this state of affairs. The constraints are as much internal as external, and this is how the women's movement appeals to those women in the professions and business who have gained formal equality with men. This too was part of the appeal of Herbert Marcuse to an affluent young generation in the late 1960s, for he showed how society limits us by getting us to limit ourselves.

So far, so good, But many liberationists over-estimate the ease with which these internal shackles can be thrown off. Some assume people to be dupes of a capitalist/male/white plot, or at least of a capitalist/male/white system, and—as people are rational—they will fight to change this once they have become aware of the situation. Education and the raising of awareness is the answer they propose. But what I want to show is how we are all *willing* dupes. We really do welcome the needs which imprison us, and we embrace them for ourselves. There are very good reasons for giving this welcome, which will not be thrown lightly aside by education or consciousness raising. And indeed it is noticeable that the educators and consciousness raisers, having debunked one set of needs, simply replace them with yet more needs; and their disciples embrace the new needs with yet more enthusiasm than the old. We cannot blame somebody else, for we are each our own jailer.

# 2: The History of Need

If needs have not always occupied a central place in human awareness, how have they been thought of in the past and when did they come to be central? This is a vast subject,[1] and I can do no more here than briefly sketch a very few lines of a complicated picture. My aim in this chapter is to show, firstly, that our own century's view of needs is far from inevitable and, secondly, to sketch the historical context in which our own views, including my own, have developed.

### Antiquity
If the twentieth-century view is that the purpose of society is to meet human needs, then the view of some of the ancient Greeks was the exact opposite. Basic needs were met by non-members of society, namely slaves and women, who were despised because of this involvement in a life of necessity. They grew and cooked the food, looked after the house, disposed of refuse, and so on; all this took place in the private household. Society was something different altogether. Society was the public arena where citizens (all male and freemen) met to discuss and argue and politick. Society was what happened *after* basic needs had been met. Far from being central to a fully human existence, needs were a diversion from it.

The Epicureans, for example, believed in pleasure, and thought that the proliferation of needs produced only a small increase in pleasure at the cost of a large increase in pain. Best therefore to limit needs. The Stoics believed it wise to concentrate on those few things over which you have control. The more needs you have, the more things affect you that you cannot control, and so for this reason it is best to limit your needs. And Favorinus, one of the Cynics, noted that 'Great needs . . . spring from great wealth; and often the best way of getting what we want is to get rid of what we have.'

Such philosophies doubtless held some truth for the minority of free citizens. But they conveniently forgot that the daily lives of over three-quarters of the people *were* preoccupied with meeting the needs of the privileged few. The philosophy rested on the assumption that those who spent their time meeting basic needs were not really human at all, or certainly not citizens of society.

The Hebrew view has already been alluded to. Things which we see as basic needs — food, health, life itself — were not seen as needs which people struggled to provide, but as blessings from a divine Creator. Rather than striving to meet our inborn lacks and needs, there is a vision in the Old Testament of a people and a land richly endowed by God. 'The Lord is my shepherd, I will not lack' (Psalm 23.1). Even when wandering in the wilderness, the very symbol of lack and need, God provided for the children of Israel so that they lacked nothing. Modern people in our so-called affluent society, brought up to strive to meet their own needs and lacks through economic or psychological effort, have great difficulty comprehending this old Hebrew concept of the original affluent society, given by God. God's gift seems to offend modern pride in human striving. We may just be able to conceive of a God who meets our needs and lacks ('Jesus will meet your every need'), but one who holds out a vision of life in which we never lack in the first place is almost beyond our comprehension. The Bible does recognize the existence of human lacks and needs, but considers them created not by God but by human beings; this is explored further in chapter 10.

The Christian Church, particularly in the writings of St Augustine, introduced a new theme: the war between the desires and needs of the flesh and the requirements of God. Not that this was the only view. Sometimes human bodily desires were seen as simply natural, as in some of St Paul's writing on marriage: marriage was necessary in order to meet the physical needs of men and women. It was therefore not to be denigrated (as the popular misunderstanding of St Paul supposes), but neither was marriage or sexual love to be spiritualized (as some nineteenth-century romantics would have it). He was concerned that, if bodily desires did not have some legitimate outlet, they might easily take a form that would conflict with the Christian life.

In other passages, Paul sees merit in subjugating bodily needs to higher purposes. He refrains from eating meat in order not to upset certain people, for he believes that the unity of the Church is more important than his penchant for veal; and fasting was a characteristic throughout Christianity, from Jesus himself onwards.

It is important to realize that the New Testament does not counterpose the needs of the body to spiritual things. There are fallen angels as well as sinful flesh; there is as much temptation in the spiritual as in the physical. But there has been throughout Christian history an awareness that the desires of the body and human will, on the one hand, and the requirements of God, on the other, may very well be in conflict. There is nothing sacrosanct about human needs. At the same time, Christian charity has been concerned to remedy human want and misery.

Christian thinking therefore has, at best, appreciated the ambiguity and complexity of human needs; at worst, been confused about them. It has varied from seeing physical needs as natural, to seeing them as spiritual dangers, to seeing them as the objects of charity. But as with the Greeks and the Hebrews, human need was never central to Christian theology. What was central was God's grace not human need. Christianity is at root God-centred, not man-centred.

## The Enlightenment

Modern notions of need draw on the kind of philosophy established by Locke in the late seventeenth century. Whereas Descartes thought that our reason was basic to human life ('I think, therefore I am'), Locke thought that desire was even more basic. Before the newborn infant gets around to thinking, he desires—food, warmth, comfort. It is through desire that he begins to relate to the world. His first conscious experience of himself is as lacking something, as needing something. He comes to know those who nurture him as those who supply that lack.

So, whereas early and medieval theology tended to see desire as spiritually dangerous, Locke and those who followed him saw it simply as the basis for all human experience, whether we like it or not. David Hume, for one, did like it. He thought that, though our wants continually multiply, our abilities multiply still faster, so we get progressively better off. He thought need to be a good basis for morality: if you *need* to do X then you *should* do X. Hume repudiated a religious foundation for morality and put in its place a foundation in human needs, interests, desires and happiness—which he called *the passions*. He observed that, though we may be totally perplexed as to the meaning of life, nevertheless most of us do get through life. In meeting the needs and desires of the body, in appeasing hunger, thirst, pain, sexual desire, we find justification enough for toil and activity. The passions provide a more effective morality for daily life than do tortuous metaphysical or religious speculations.[2]

In the nineteenth century other philosophers, such as Bentham and Mill, developed these ideas which clearly meshed with the experience of the ruling class of a Britain that was expanding economically and coming to dominate the world politically. In general, it was deemed to be progress to move from the basic natural needs to higher, and in a sense artificial, needs; certainly industrial Britain required ever more needs in order to expand.

Some of the early socialists were not sure about this, though. They clearly distinguished basic needs, which are natural and not influenced (so they thought) by society, and which are the basis for human beings coming together in society, from artificial needs which were created by a technology and a rampant capitalism that had got out of control. This approach tended to romanticize primitive peoples. Rousseau thought that once simple, natural needs are met, people begin to procure all kinds of conveniences unknown to their forefathers. So far so good, but then these conveniences become real needs in the sense that it is more painful to be without them than pleasant to have them. If only they remained wants, all would be well; but when they turn into needs, we store up trouble for ourselves. In particular, we are prone to exploitation by those who provide our needs; we become entangled in a complex, exploitative society.

The German philosopher Hegel made some crucial connections that rendered some of our twentieth-century views possible. He started with the observation that, in themselves, people are not self-sufficient. They have to create their own sufficiency by struggling to meet their needs; in this struggle with the external, natural world they become aware of themselves. Without the struggle, they would have no self-awareness; and without the needs, there would be no struggle. This is what both history and our dealings with the

14

natural world are all about. Unlike Rousseau, who saw this need for self-estimation and for esteem from others as creating all kinds of false needs and exploitation by others, Hegel saw it as precisely the means by which the knots of society are tied. For Hegel, society is a system of needs.

The way in which need enters into Marx's writings is quite complex and varied.[3] Suffice it to say here that on the one hand there is an echo of Hegel. Needs are the cement of society, and Marx's envisioned communist society — 'to each according to his need' — fulfils Hegel's vision. On the other hand, Marx draws from the early socialists the distinction between true and false needs, though for him this is not the same as the distinction between natural and artificial needs. He is aware both that the experience of even the most basic needs is influenced by the society one lives in, and that many higher 'cultural' needs may be highly desirable. To have criteria for knowing what are true needs is essential if the slogan 'to each according to his need' is to mean very much.

In these philosophers lie the seeds of much of the present-day talk about needs. The utilitarians had a view of needs not so different from that of many modern businessmen, advertisers and economists who believe economic growth to be a healthy response to the ever-expanding needs of human beings. The primitivist Rousseau heralds those today who long to get back to the simple life not dependent on modern technology, and who dub primitive needs as 'natural'. Hegel foreshadows those existentialists and humanists who see the development of the personality as a process of 'becoming'. And Marx's concern for identifying our true needs was rediscovered in the 1960s by many students.

## The Twentieth Century

It was not until this century, however, that these ideas — basically, that the human project is the progressive meeting of our needs — came to be deeply rooted in the everyday experience of ordinary men and women. In this section, I will suggest four features of the modern world since 1945 that seem to me to have helped carry these ideas into everyday life and language. They are: (i) the absorption of psychological ideas into everyday experience; (ii) the welfare state; (iii) the United Nations; and (iv) the consumer society. Let's look briefly at each.

15

*Psychology*

Freud shared with St Paul an understanding of the inevitable conflict between instinctual desires (the id) and the conscience (the super-ego). He saw both civilization and the more pathological parts of our personalities as the result of the sublimation or repression of the id. The complexity and subtlety of his theory, however, is understood by few; what *has* been taken from Freud by millions of people is the simplistic notion that it is bad to repress our sexual and other basic emotional needs. People have adopted Freud's notion that the gratification of our needs is what motivates all human behaviour, but have lost sight of his understanding of how creative can be the struggle between those needs and the conscience and the will.

It seems likely that mid-twentieth-century culture has used Freud as much as it has been shaped by him. There is a part of Freud that fits our notion of human needs, and so he has been wheeled in to give intellectual credence to it. From all great teachers, people hear what they want to hear.

The notion of need was also adopted by other psychologists for a brief period in the 1920s. They thought that basic physiological needs provided an objective starting point for psychology, a starting point on which everyone could agree and where language was unambiguous. But fairly soon it became apparent that, especially with sexual and other more complex needs, experts were not at all agreed, and the word *need* was abandoned in favour of *drive*. Unlike needs, which had been believed to be real deficits residing in the individual, drives were recognized as no more than a useful unobservable construct that psychologists could employ to help make sense of behaviour they *could* observe. But the belief that human behaviour is motivated by basic needs or drives has remained influential in psychology ever since. From the 1940s onwards, this was combined with a belief in progress to produce the humanistic psychologies of Maslow, Rogers, Fromm and others, in which the person advances from basic needs to ever higher needs, a view which has been profoundly influential on the psychiatric couches of middle-class America. Needs imply lacks; we are born empty and incomplete. We are potential only, and life is the striving to fill up the emptiness and become more complete. Self-actualization, realizing our full potential, becomes the goal of life.

## The welfare state

In North America, psychology has been a major channel through which the notion of need has entered everyday life. In Britain, perhaps the introduction of the welfare state has been more influential; this has meant that meeting people's needs has displayed an altruistic rather than a self-centred flavour, meeting your needs as well as mine. But the basic notion is the same: civilization as the progressive meeting of human need.

Following the Second World War, there was tremendous popular support for establishing and developing a tax-supported health service, schooling, social security and other welfare services. We may not have been so very sure what we had been fighting for in the war, but we united under the banner of a nation that looked after the needs of its people. With religion no longer providing any national purpose and with liberal capitalism having shown itself bankrupt in the depression of the 1930s, what universal values were there that could direct national life? The answer was clear, and has been clear to those left of centre ever since. 'The universal satisfaction of vital needs and, beyond it, the progressive alleviation of toil and poverty are universally valid standards.' That was said by Herbert Marcuse, and is the goal of paternalist socialism the world over.

## The United Nations

Something similar was happening on the international scene, though without the rhetoric of socialism. The United Nations was set up because there had to be some kind of international forum for the nations to resolve their differences *before* things got to the stage of another world war. But what was it that would enable nations to get together, what was it that would unite them? The answer came in the form of two related slogans — human rights and human needs. All human beings, irrespective of nationality or politics, it was proposed, had certain rights that had to be safeguarded and certain basic needs that had to be met if they were to be able to lead fully human lives. Many of the United Nations' subsidiary organizations are devoted to those groups most in danger of

17

their rights and needs not being met, like children (UNICEF, UNESCO), the sick (WHO), and the hungry (FAO). Making sure that everyone's needs for health services, education, employment, food and so on are met is the goal that unites member states of very different political persuasions. Or that at least is the hope.

The problem in a century marked by the Gulag and the Holocaust was how to find a common and universally acceptable basis for human dignity. On what could human rights rest? Clearly, religious beliefs were of no avail, for the member states of the United Nations were of many religions and of none. But they did all pay lip service to science, and so it seemed fruitful to try to base human dignity on facts rather than on values. Facts are universal, values manifestly are not. And what fact about human existence is most obvious, or obvious at least to post-Lockian, post-Enlightenment, humankind? The fact that we are all born with needs; needs which must be met if we are to know anything like a decent life; needs which must be met if we are to have any chance of fulfilling our potential. An undernourished peasant child will never grow to be a worker able to contribute properly to society; a child who is not loved will be emotionally handicapped for life. So the meeting of human needs became the basis without which human dignity was hardly possible. It seemed that human rights could be based on objective fact, and a vast army of scientists and social scientists was commissioned by WHO, UNESCO and the rest to establish with greater and greater precision the needs of human beings and how to meet them. Human dignity, and ultimately world peace, had been reduced to a technical problem.

### The consumer society

The programmes for meeting human need pioneered by psychologists, socialist politicians and international organi-zations provided good reason for the vast expansion of welfare bureaucracies and welfare professions (doctors, teachers, social workers, and so on). But big business was not averse to such programmes either. They welcomed anything that brought the poor into the markets for education, health and basic consumer durables that had previously been the preserve of a middle class minority, for it became apparent that capitalism's future depended on everyone, not just a

18

wealthy minority, becoming consumers. Advertisements quickly adopted the new language of need. If scientists are agreed that need is what drives your life and mine, then clearly anyone with something to sell had to demonstrate that people needed it. So it was that every product became a need.

In the radical sixties, criticism of the consumer society revived the old nineteenth-century socialist concern with distinguishing true from false needs. The consumer society generated lots of false needs, indeed it depended on generating them in order continually to expand; critics of the consumer society set themselves the task of somehow working out what were people's real needs. To do this, they required some understanding of human nature and human fulfilment, and so they turned to various Freudian and humanistic psychologies of the 'self-actualization' variety, thus linking the old European socialist tradition of 'to each according to his need' with the American preoccupation with psychiatry. Several New Left gurus, like Marcuse and Fromm, were European émigrés living in the United States. They succeeded in articulating dissatisfaction with consumerism, but at the cost of alluding to yet more psychological needs, which big business was hardly slow in capitalizing on! Which perhaps demonstrates the power not only of the consumer society, but also of our apparent need for needs.

At the heart of the consumer society is the language of need. This language is so deeply rooted that even consumerism's most strident critics have used the language of need in their attack on consumerism. I doubt whether such attacks can work in the long run, because the language of need is as much the problem as is the consumer society.

The New Left's revival of a vision of a society that meets our true needs was a reaction not only to post-war consumer society, but also to the belief of social scientists in the 1950s that their academic studies should be value-free, objective and scientific. They felt their work as social scientists to be in the realm of facts, of what *is* the case, and that this had to be separated from their role as responsible citizens where they were allowed to use the language of what *ought* to be. While there was no logical reason why this separation of *is* and *ought* statements should have inhibited moral and ethical declarations of value in the appropriate places, in practice it did.[4] Radical social scientists, who passionately *did* want to make statements of value, latched onto the concept of need as the way through this impasse, for a need is both a scientifically demonstrable fact *and* it carries imperative force. This is what radical social scientists like C. Wright Mills and Herbert Marcuse had in common with the average bureaucrat or research scientist in the United Nations.

But we no longer live in the heady days of the radical sixties when a buoyant economy could support buoyant critics. The early 1980s have seen the biggest worldwide depression since the 1930s, and it has become as easy to see through the extravagance of the psychological needs proclaimed by West Coast psychotherapists as it is for the unemployed to see the obscenity of consumer needs from which they are excluded for lack of funds. If you have learnt to do without a car and to forego redecorating the living room even though it badly needs it, then you will have certainly learnt to do without autonomy and self-actualization! What autonomy is there anyway without money? Self-actualization is no longer plausible as a need, a goal for everyone; once again it becomes a luxury for the rich.

This is the context in which I am writing and maybe too in which you are reading this book. Not that either I or perhaps you are currently unemployed, but both of us are probably limiting our horizons and our purses, and it is easier to become critical of the fad for needs now it is so obvious that most of them cannot be met. Economic depression has surely made it easier for me, and perhaps for you too, to think critically about the language of needs.

# PART ONE
# A WORLD IN NEED

# 3: Material Needs

We are plagued by materialism, the Jeremiahs tell us. In some conservative pulpits, it is the chief sin of the age along with sexual permissiveness. Environmentalists complain of the rape of planet earth by the rich nations. Governments, especially but not uniquely those of the right, consider workers in general and the trade unions in particular to be motivated by selfish greed in what governments consider excessive wage claims. And those a little left of centre who are concerned about the international division of the riches of the world continually point the finger at the greed and selfishness of the first and second worlds in their dealings with the third.

Although *other* people's material wants are often declaimed as materialistic and excessive in their craving for luxuries, no one ever considers their own purchases as selfish, greedy or materialistic. In fact, if you listen to your own and others' justifications for their various purchases, it is need and not greed that is continually referred to. And not cynically, nor tongue in cheek. You and they and I really mean it. And that includes the wealthiest people in the wealthiest nations (which probably includes you, dear reader, for you are most likely in the top 10 per cent of the world's spenders). Has anyone ever said, 'I feel like getting some new golf clubs'? It is always, 'I need a new set of clubs'. On those rare occasions when we do not see a purchase as a necessity, we usually feel we have to justify it either to ourselves or to others; the implication of this is that the normal reason for spending is need, and any other reason must be justified.

Many of these needs are not our own. They are the needs of wife or husband, the needs of our children: 'The children need new shoes'; 'Alice needs a bag for school'; 'Jim needs a new suit for work'; 'Marjory needs a night out'. The charge of greedy materialism is doubly mistaken here. Consumers are motivated not by greedy avarice but by a sense of need; and furthermore, they see their expenditure as not on their own needs but on the needs of their loved ones.

Looked at from the outside, looking at the expenditure of others, what one sees is *households* spending on themselves.

This is what the directors of international relief agencies see, and undoubtedly Western householders *are* greedy at the expense of the Third World. (Economists, too, generally look at the expenditure of households rather than at the expenditure of individuals.) But when you get inside the household, what you see is not a household spending on itself, but individuals spending on their loved ones: parents spending on their children, and spouses and lovers spending on each other. A rather small portion of purchases are made by people for themselves. Most of the goods wheeled out of the supermarket will be consumed by other members of the purchaser's family. The husband may be possessive about who drives 'his' car, but many of his journeys he experiences as giving to others, like giving his wife a lift to work, or taking the family on vacation. The wife has a similar attitude to the car, and many of her journeys are spent ferrying the children around.[1] The husband may genuinely enjoy assembling a do-it-yourself kitchen, but he does not experience this as a hobby, but as something done 'for the wife — she needs a new kitchen, and this is the only way we can afford it'. So it is that family members see their own purchases as motivated by need and by love, but when they look at other households from the outside they see only greed. And the further away you get from the household — as in statements from pulpits and political rostrums about the masses — the more obscene greed appears.

This is why governments' pleas for wage restraint and sacrifices so often fall on deaf ears. The government thinks it is asking individuals to spend a little less on themselves, which indeed would be restraint and a sacrifice. But in fact it is asking individuals to spend less on others, which means a husband failing in his duty as breadwinner for his family, or it means a working mother failing to provide adequately for her children. Far from a worthy sacrifice, this is seen by the worker as *im*moral. Those who make the sacrifice are the worker's dependants — the young mother, the children, the elderly, the sick and the handicapped — but what politician would dare ask *them* to make a sacrifice?

Those who try to raise money for charities face a similar problem. It is no good appealing to the ethical worth of giving to the world's poor in contrast to the selfishness of spending on ourselves, because that is not how we see our spending. Rather, the contrast is between giving to the anonymous poor of the world and spending on our own loved ones, and it is clear to all which is the moral priority. The man who says, 'Sorry, pal, but charity begins at home,' and puts nothing in the collecting tin is not making a feeble excuse; he has in fact put his finger exactly on what motivates most household spending.

So, far from being greedy, we see ourselves as giving to meet the needs of others. Now this *may* constitute greed and materialism according to some moral code or according to some norm of international justice (it does seem greedy in a way to buy your child a new pair of shoes when millions of children go barefoot), but greed and materialism is *not* what *motivates* consumers in the Western world. What motivates us, mostly, is necessity and love.

The morality of our motives is quite subtle. Rejecting the charge of selfishness, we defend ourselves by saying—truly —that we do not see most of our purchases as either moral or immoral. They are simply necessities. We must have a place to live; we must have food; our children must have clothes—and these are the kinds of things that make up most of our spending. And yet need is not ethically neutral, and part of us knows that too. If the children need new shoes, then they *must* have them. Need is not just a statement of fact, it also provides an imperative. It justifies the purchase. It is a *good* reason, a very good reason.[2]

Don't get me wrong. It is a very fine thing that mundane activities like cooking a meal, shopping, or repainting the kitchen should be offered as love-gifts to our loved ones. But it is precisely this that enables us to put such mundane things above moral evaluation; they are so manifestly good that any other competing demands on our purse are seen as less than loving or loving less important people. Hence the paltry sums that go into the charity tin.

So need takes the purchase and consumption of goods out of the old court of moral appeal, where there was much talk of greed and selfishness, and puts it into a new court. It provides a new moral framework for consumption. It kicks traditional moral categories out of the front door, while quietly letting new forms of justification in at the back door.

## Needs and Luxuries

Another feature of how people talk of other people's spending is to distinguish luxuries from needs. 'Look at that new furniture the Jones have bought. They can't possibly afford it, and they don't need it anyway.' 'Jim and Jane have just moved to a luxurious new house.' And certainly an Indian peasant looking at our Western lifestyle would see luxury a-plenty. But ask Jim and Jane and they would say the house simply meets their needs better than the old one, and the Jones really *do* think they need new furnishings.

We rarely experience our own lifestyle as luxurious. Occasionally we like a little luxury, but that is a rare treat to be treasured. We may long for the day when we can afford a few luxuries, but somehow that day never comes, for by then the luxuries have become necessities. The notion that, once we have met our basic needs, we may then move into the realm of luxuries is a lie, just as it is a lie to suppose that once a person's basic emotional and psychological needs have been met he may then begin to act in freedom. Once people enter the prison of needs, they are never released.

A good example of how luxuries quickly become needs is provided by the automobile. When mass car ownership first became a possibility in a nation, the advertising showed how the car would provide freedom. This was how Henry Ford sold his cars in the 1920s — at long last Americans could explore for themselves the great outdoors that was their birthright as Americans. It is also how popular models have been advertised in Britain since the war; small cars for families of modest income are pictured most often in some wild or romantic setting, with the clear message that the car provides freedom to escape the city and mundane life. Indeed, this is how many people experience their first car purchase. They do not need it, but it is nice to be able to take the wife and kids for a drive at weekends. They genuinely buy the car in freedom.

But almost inevitably they come to be dependent on it. The first slide into dependence may be a move of house. Having the car, they are not so concerned that the new house be within easy walking or bus distance from work, shops, and school, and the result is that they put themselves into a position where they need the car. The ensuing months witness a further slide. A whole range of social contacts is built up, for children as well as parents, on the basis of the car, which becomes even more of a necessity. The final straw comes when so many people follow this pattern that the demand for public transport declines and services are withdrawn; town planners, supermarket chains and employers assume car ownership to be the norm, and it becomes impossible to conduct a viable life without the car.

This is a good example of an addictive need. Unlike the unthinking assumption that the need comes first, and then its satisfaction, actually the reverse is the case with addictive needs. First comes the satisfaction (going out to the country in the car on a Sunday), *then* comes the need (life is not viable without the car). People can see this with others' addictions, notably something like heroin addiction, but are blind to the fact that many of their own needs are of this kind.


**Creating Need**

How have we come to this state of affairs in which needs expand continuously, without any noticeable increase in satisfaction?

Certainly it has not always been so. In the eighteenth century, 'the labouring poor' were those who earned enough by their labour to satisfy their daily wants at the standard appropriate to their class, but no more, and so they had to go on working. It was generally assumed that their wants were static; so if they were allowed to earn any more, then the motive for work would cease and they would grow idle. Bernard Mandeville, writing in 1714, commented that the labourers 'have nothing to stir them up to be serviceable but their Wants, which it is Prudence to relieve, but Folly to cure'.[3]

Clearly things had changed by 1844 when Karl Marx wrote of how capitalism thrived on the continual creation of new wants and needs:

Under private property . . . every person speculates on creating a new need in another, so as to drive him to a fresh sacrifice, place him in a new dependence and to seduce him into a new mode of gratification and therefore economic ruin. Each tries to establish over the other an alien power, so as thereby to find satisfaction of his own selfish need. The increase in the quantity of objects is accompanied by an extension of the realm of the alien powers to which man is subjected, and every new product represents a new possibility of mutual swindling and mutual plundering. Man becomes ever poorer as man, his need for money becomes ever greater if he wants to overpower hostile beings. The power of his money declines so to say in inverse proportion to the increase in the volume of production: that is, his neediness grows as the power of money increases.[4]

If these two authors are to be believed, something had happened between 1714 and 1844, for the needs of the common people had ceased to be static and had set foot on a continual escalator. What was the cause of the change? What keeps the escalator going today? Is it capitalism as Marx thought? Or an inevitable consequence of technology, or of industrialization? How are material needs generated today? There is still no agreement over the answer to these questions. Various theories help us understand how needs have got onto an escalator; what none of them help us understand is why people actually want to be on such an escalator.[5] Let's consider some of the possibilities.

It certainly does happen that technology can breed new needs. The American space programme saw several technological innovations for which entrepreneurs then searched for a wider and more enduring market. Each innovation provided a solution in search of a problem. And so it was that householders came to need non-stick saucepans, and backpackers to need emergency lightweight space blankets. Often this is not a matter of avaricious and cunning advertisers; it may simply be that scientists have found a wonderful new toy, and understandably they want to do something with it and find some use for it.

Technology does not explain anything like all our modern needs for goods, however. There is no inherent reason why consumers should be as enamoured as the scientists with the new toy, and one certainly hears less of space blankets and non-stick saucepans nowadays. Or, a major consumer may decide explicitly to reject a technology. North Americans decided that they did not want a supersonic airliner; the means was there to travel at twice the speed of sound, but they simply did not see the need, or they felt the environmental price was to high. Technology may sometimes lead to new needs, but there is nothing inevitable about this. The flushing toilet was invented three hundred years before it came into general use.

It is easy to think that consumer needs are created by advertising, that the masses are like sheep, led hither and thither by the wiles of the advertisers. There is in fact very little evidence that this happens. There are too many examples of major advertising campaigns that have been complete flops. Advertising itself is a stressful occupation, precisely because the advertisers themselves know they cannot predict for sure what kinds of slogan will sell their goods. There is no magic potion that will make anything a best seller. I know all too well that in the publishing business there are formula books which are commissioned and that the publisher knows will sell, but there is no way a publisher can commission a best seller. If there were, there would be many more rich authors!

Many advertisers would say that, far from creating new needs, they simply respond to needs that already exist. Market research partly involves discovering what unmet needs exist, and tailoring one's product to meet those needs. Manufacturers often genuinely see themselves in the business of meeting, not creating, need, and this is part of the satisfaction of the job. Rather few people can work for long dreaming up totally spurious reasons why people should buy an utterly useless product; it is certainly hard to be enthusiastic about a product that you yourself are cynical about, and without enthusiasm on the part of the designers and advertisers the product is hardly likely to sell.

If advertisers and designers believe they are meeting needs, and critics believe they are manufacturing needs, I suspect the truth lies somewhere in between. Advertising has to appeal to needs that people already feel, for example for love, belonging, prestige, identity, or escape, and then proceed to show how the product will meet one or more of these needs, so that the product itself becomes needed. Advertising *does* create needs, but not out of nothing. It confirms the needs we already feel.[6] The automobile advertisement that depicts a family car drawn off the road in an idyllic mountain location relies on some pre-existing need or desire to escape to the peace and calm of nature, and then informs us that we need a certain model of car to do this; but in so doing reaffirms that the need to escape is indeed an authentic need.

An explanation that may help account for the proliferation of material needs in the mid-twentieth century is that they are the result of the economic policies conducted by most governments since the 1930s. Before then, thrift was a powerful motive in most people's lives. Thrift and saving were the means by which capital was available for investment, and it was the only way that the poor could feel any confidence that they would be able to see themselves through bad times and avoid a pauper's funeral. So thrift was highly functional for those who lived through the industrial revolution. Views changed, however, as a result of the Great Depression of the 1930s. The old policy of individuals, firms and nations tightening their belts in order to see themselves through the depression was clearly not working, as it was taking more and more money out of the economy, reducing demand, and deepening the recession. Keynes' revolutionary answer was to spend our way out of depression; if somehow demand could be artificially stimulated, jobs would be created, people would have more money to spend and the economy would get going again. As it happened, rearmament and the war achieved all this anyway, but the general Keynesian approach has influenced all post-war Western governments. Only recently, in the recession of the early 1980s, has the Keynesian tradition been broken by the deflationary policies of Margaret Thatcher.

However, in the meantime governments had a formidable task on their hands. Respectable working people had for generations been practising thrift and believed it irresponsible to spend beyond their means. Somehow they had to be got to spend without feeling guilty. Advanced capitalism required people to be greedy if it was to continue to expand, yet it had bred generation after generation that disapproved of greed. The answer was to portray the new consumerism as a matter of spending to meet need rather than spending to meet greed. Which is not to say that manufacturers or advertisers or economic policies could create specific needs, but that the language of need replaced the language of greed in the market place.

Along with the language of need went talk of rights. In the 1950s the British premier Harold Macmillan, with his slogan of 'You've never had it so good', helped generate the feeling that after the sacrifices of the war, the depression and decades of industrial grime and poverty, the British people had earned the right to a life of abundance. It was their birthright. And certainly they owed it to their children that they should never again need for anything.

This alliance between economists, politicians and business succeeded in changing the language of consumption. Consuming was a good thing now, and the needs that gave rise to it hardly less good than the goods which satisfied the needs. Hardly surprising then, that governments of the 1970s and 1980s have pleaded in vain for wage restraint. Having spent two decades educating people that spending was a good thing, they suddenly backtracked; by then, people had lost the values of the 1930s and earlier, the values of thrift and of 'making do'. It is perhaps possible to have a stop-go economic policy that invisibly brakes and accelerates the economy every two or three years, but to play around in a stop-go fashion with the deepest economic motives of the whole population is bound to create trouble.

More important, though, than the language of need is the way in which many more goods have actually become necessary. Crucial here is the de-skilling that has been going on ever since the industrial revolution. There has been much talk of the de-skilling of the worker by machines, but of equal importance has been the re-skilling of the consumer. All kinds of goods were once made by the household that used them: houses, clothes, toys, kitchen utensils. Such goods may have been crude and people may have been poor, but they had the satisfaction of producing many of the necessities of life for themselves. But with the arrival of cheap, mass-produced goods, the skills that once enabled people to make do on their own no longer have any use. Many of these manufactured goods are cheaper to replace than to mend once they have worn out—you can darn woollen stockings but not a pair of nylon tights. The consumer has developed new skills—deciphering technical information in order to be able to choose between a hundred-and-one varieties of commodity—but these skills enable us to meet our needs for consumer goods, not to abolish them. We have changed from being skilled producers to being skilled consumers. This is what Ivan Illich has called the new poverty, for in the midst of a cornucopia of glossy goods and apparent abundance, we have forfeited the inner wealth of many of our own productive skills.

This is even true of something like motherhood. In previous generations a girl learned how to mother by watching her own mother with her younger brothers and sisters, and she could practise on them herself. Now with smaller families, more isolated perhaps from neighbours and kin, she can grow into adulthood without ever having touched a baby. At the same time, motherhood is rated very highly. So she becomes dependent on the vast baby industry, from books on babycare to the health services, and in her insecurity she relies on fancy prams and special baby foods to convince herself and others that she loves her baby and is caring for it properly.

So, all our needs today have to be met by commodities. The system takes our skills from us and sells them back to us for the price of a commodity. And yet each commodity never quite satisfies, and more commodities are needed.

Proportionately many more goods and services used to be exchanged informally among friends, families and neighbours, for free or as a favour to be returned some time. Trust, co-operation, mutual obligation, love, service—these were the motives that lay behind such exchanges. But with the breakdown of many of the old neighbourhoods, many such exchanges are no longer possible; such goods and services now have to be bought and sold on the open market, where the motive of profitability reigns supreme. Insofar as the old informal exchanges continue, as they do in some places, they are frowned upon by the tax-collector, and some such exchanges are derogatorily labelled by economists as 'the black economy'. For those outside this informal economy, the only arena left in which love and mutual obligation rather than profit cover the provision of goods and services, is the private family, which most economists do not consider at all.[7] Karl Marx was never more apposite to today than when he wrote:

Finally, there came a time when everything that men had considered as inalienable became an object of exchange, of traffic, and could be alienated. This is the time when the very things which till then had been communicated, but never exchanged; given, but never sold;

acquired, but never bought — virtue, love, conviction, knowledge, conscience, etc. — when everything, in short, passed into commerce. It is the time of general corruption, of universal venality.[8]

Knowledge now has to be paid for by taxes through the education service; it is no longer picked up for free as father hands down skills to son, mother to daughter. Neighbourliness has to be paid for in the form of a social worker. Even mother-love cannot be given without the aid of dozens of purchases from the babycare industry.

### Scarcity as Ideology

What we have here is the creation of scarcity. Curiously, economics, the science that is devoted to the study of the supply and demand of goods and services, does not see scarcity in this light at all. Instead it assumes that the scarcity of goods and services is an inevitable part of the human lot, something given rather than created by human beings. Virtually all economics textbooks start from this so-called universal fact of scarcity, for example: 'Scarcity: a condition which mankind perpetually faces because at any moment in time total resources are fixed.'[9] This is blithely stated by professors of economics, in ignorance of anthropology, history, theology, and ecology, all of which suggest that the experience of scarcity is not the inevitable or original lot of mankind. Let us briefly review what these other disciplines have to say.

The anthropologist Marshall Sahlins in his *Stone Age Economics*[10] provides evidence that primitive hunter-gatherer tribes are not usually pre-occupied by a struggle for food. Where the climate is favourable, they may spend as little as two hours a day searching for food, and it is far from their experience that food is scarce. The evidence is not absolutely unequivocal, but certainly there is no justification for blithely assuming that the basic necessities of human life have been, are, and ever will be scarce.

It is not surprising, therefore, that the myths and religions of primitive societies sometimes picture a world of abundance rather than of necessity. One of the most complete records we have of the religion of a simple agricultural society is the Old Testament. There, humankind's original state is the abundance of the Garden of Eden, richly endowed by a Creator God. Even after man's fall, the promise to the children of Israel is to occupy a land flowing with milk and honey—this is no never-never land or golden past age which nobody actually inhabited, but how their religion depicted the land they actually lived in. Their view of economics was premised on this abundance; tithing, giving away a tenth of the produce, was possible even in lean years because of faith in the basic abundance of creation. When scarcity did occur, it was usually seen as anomalous—the people complained to their Maker, and the prophets told them the scarcity was due to the people's sin. Prophet and people may have disagreed as to the cause of a famine or poor harvest, but both agreed that it ought not to have happened. Scarcity was something artificially constructed, by either God or man; it was not natural.

Contrast this with the 'basic-needs' approach to world development that became fashionable among United Nations economists in the 1970s.[11] They believed human beings to have universal physical needs which must be identified, and the economic priorities of poor nations (often with agricultural economies similar to those of ancient Israel) should be geared toward meeting them, starting with the most basic needs and then working upwards. Though the needs, broadly defined, are universal, in any particular nation it is the people themselves who should assess their basic needs. This, the economists feel, is difficult because the people lack knowledge, and what knowledge they do have may come from the wrong sources, like Coca-Cola telling them that consuming junk drink is a mark of sophistication and Westernization.

But the problem is much deeper: the people themselves may not even see themselves as having a hierarchy of needs. They may actually have something to teach us in the way in which they put other things (like religion or loyalty to kin or simple amusements) before food and shelter, and in the way they can experience as plenty what to a Westerner seems scarcity. This is not to deny that starvation, leprosy and drought are terrible things. It is simply to question whether Western concepts of need and scarcity will help people to rid themselves of such scourges, still less help them to bear whatever suffering remains.

Allied to anthropology and Old Testament theology is the view of some modern ecologists. For them, this is an abundant planet and it is we human beings who have created scarcities out of abundance. For the ecologists, the economists' view of scarcity 'implies that nature has failed to endow our planet richly enough'. (Replace 'nature' with 'Yahweh' and you have precisely the prophets' charge against the children of Israel when in bad times their faith deserted them.) The alternative view of some socialist ecologists is that 'scarcity may be regarded as stemming from an allocation of abundant resources in a wasteful, unjust, and irrational manner'.[12]

Why then do modern economists assume scarcity to be inherent in human experience? I do not know. But it is clear what the effect of this assumption is. It affirms that the scarcity we experience daily in our modern Western lives is natural, inevitable, and therefore proper. It affirms that scarcity is given, a basic fact of life, instead of constructed by the very system that purports to meet it. This profound lie is at the heart of economics. And the effect is to say that our present system of needs is ordained, not by capitalism, by socialism or by modern industrialism, but by the human condition itself. So economics, the discipline devoted to understanding material wants and how people meet them, is unfitted from the very start for that task. It is unable to rise above the very view of needs which it must rise above if it is to examine needs objectively.

Further evidence that economists share the same concept of need with the system they are supposed to be studying is provided by their concept of 'consumer sovereignty'. They assume the demands, preferences and needs of consumers to be autonomous, independent variables which arise out of nowhere other than, presumably, the free choice of the individual consumer. Like the shopkeeper who claims to be solely devoted to serving the needs of the customer, by ignoring the source of consumer preferences the economist *de facto* treats the consumer as God and his choices as uncreated. His expressed needs, in the form of demand, are part of the basic, unquestionable, data with which the economist proceeds.[13]

Not only do economists fail to ask where the consumer's needs come from, they also do not ask what his needs are *for*. A person always needs something for a purpose, and it is the validity or otherwise of the purpose that logically makes the need valid or not. 'I need a car.' What for? To take my family on vacation? To take me to work? To get away after robbing a bank? To show up my neighbours who can't afford one? Clearly the legitimacy of my need for a car depends on what purpose it serves. In practice, people usually do not ask of a need 'What for?' unless they wish to query the need. That economists do not ask 'What for?' means that they too implicitly affirm the legitimacy of *all* material needs.

Economists will doubtless reply that they do not ask questions such as where needs come from and what they are for, because such issues are not necessary for understanding the mechanisms of the market; they are questions that are at best peripheral to, at worst outside the domain of, economics. Perhaps so; and certainly, if economists say such questions are outside the domain of economics, then clearly they *are* outside the domain of economics. But the result, for better or for worse, is that economics cannot query the creation of needs in modern society and implicitly, but strongly, affirms all material needs to be good and equal. Which is getting very near to materialism; ordinary consumers may not be materialistic, but economics certainly seems to be.

Economists also assume that needs continually expand. This is not considered a pathological result of our present society, nor a process in which it is in some people's interests that other people's needs should expand and increase their dependence. It is not corporate business, or capitalism, or sin that makes needs expand, but that abstract entity 'man'. As one best-selling textbook puts it: 'For all practical purposes, human wants may be regarded as limitless. An occasional individual may have everything he wants, but man's capacity to create new wants as fast as he satisfies old ones is well-known psychologically.'[14]

That needs expand is, therefore, unquestionable. And again, a right-wing English politician, Sir Keith Joseph: 'Our experience of market society shows that needs expand *pari passu* with possibilities, if not faster.' At least Sir Keith appreciates that the phenomenon may be limited to market society, and may not be the lot of all humans, but since there is no real alternative to some form of market society (even the Soviets have a modified form of market economy) he too is justifying the continual escalation of needs.

This little excursion into economics is not intended to knock economics in itself. I am a sociologist by training, and goodness knows, sociologists should not throw stones; they too live in glasshouses. No, the aim is simply to show that so deep-rooted is the modern experience of needs that even the scientific discipline studying people's material wants and their supply starts from *within* the modern framework of needs, unable or unwilling to view it from the outside. In the next chapter I want to show that the same is true of much psychology.

# 4: The Needs of the Self

What is the self? Who, and what, am I?

Throughout most human history, people have understood themselves in a social way. They had self-respect and respect from others if they faithfully played out the particular social roles allotted to them, if they knew themselves to be and were known to be a good farmer, a devoted wife, a conscientious mother, a reliable craftsman, a loyal communist, or whatever. Doing one's duty in one's allotted role was what life was all about. Ask somebody who he was, and the reply might be: 'I'm a farmer, Mary's husband and the father of five children, though I find it hard providing for them all.' His identity *was* his social roles plus his competence or lack of it in doing what was required of him in those roles, that is, his duty.

Also, many human beings have understood themselves in a religious way. They saw their actions as offending or placating the spirits; they saw themselves and were seen by others as morally good / a faithful Christian / devout Moslem, or were cast out as moral reprobates; they saw their inner self as the site of a spiritual conflict, between flesh and spirit, body and soul, desire and conscience. St Paul's experience of himself has been echoed by millions of Christians since:

When I want to do right, evil lies close at hand. For I delight in the law of God, in my inmost self, but I see in my members another law at war with the law of my mind and making me captive to the law of sin which dwells in my members . . . I of myself serve the law of God with my mind, but with my flesh I serve the law of sin.[1]

These religious and social self-conceptions can be illustrated by motherhood and work. Throughout history, people have wanted children and most have wanted to work, but the reasons have varied. In many traditional societies, a childless woman had little part to play in the community; she needed children because without them she would not be a full member of society. And of course most women have had little option but to have children. Likewise, most people have had little option but to work for their living. Sometimes work was

38

also experienced religiously, as a calling from God, as for example with the Puritans of the sixteenth century.

People still work and bear and rear children, but the motive is no longer seen as purely of social or divine origin; it is believed increasingly to come from within. Less obligated to God or to society, the free individual of modern democracies has invented a new obligation—to himself or herself. If duty is spoken of at all today, it is the duty to oneself. The woman feels she must have children if she is to fulfil herself as a woman; this femininity is something within herself, not a part to play in either God's or society's drama. Though most people work in order to fulfil their duty to support their family, that is, to enact the social role of breadwinner, and many of the unemployed feel a failure because they are unable to do this ('I promised to support her and all that, and I'm not'), there is growing alongside this a rhetoric of work as meeting some of the individual's basic psychological needs.

The individual himself or herself, and his closest loved ones, are seen as a person's ultimate frame of reference, and meeting the needs of the self is increasingly talked of as life's project. Social and religious experiences of the self are replaced by a psychological conception in which 'the human self is a hierarchy of inner needs and self-fulfilment an inner journey to discover them'.[2] The me that was once an assemblage of social roles is now an assemblage of inner needs. I see myself as driven not by social norms or by divine command, but by inner necessities. We still feel the weight of social obligations. But, increasingly, personal needs have become the currency for talking about undoubtedly social behaviour. That inner needs now supplement social norms and religious ethics shows the essentially *moral* nature of psychological needs. The childless woman or unemployed man today feels a personal failure as much as a social failure, but that they feel they have failed is constant; motherhood and work are moral activities in face of this psychological need, and therefore to abstain from them is immoral.

Such, it seems, is the ethos of our time. Clearly I have overdrawn the picture. The unemployed person today is barred from participation in society—no social life at work, no self respect and no income, none of the prerequisites for entering social life—in much the same way as the childless woman often was in past societies. The picture is most accurate in those places where social and religious norms have become most relaxed, leaving a vacuum to be filled only by the individual and his needs.

The view of the self as a package of inner needs first gained wide currency in California in the 1950s and 1960s, a society where affluence had lifted many out of some of the old constraints, and high mobility had detached people from old networks of kin, stable neighbourhoods and traditional church life. In the privacy of their suburban ranch houses, this affluent class was perhaps as detached from the demands of society as any in history. What then could guide their lives?

To their rescue came humanistic psychology. Many of these restless people suffered the neurotic disorders of their mobile lifestyle; the more desperate and affluent of them turned to their psychiatrists, while the rest perused the mushrooming number of books on pop psychology. (To my British eyes it is intriguing to find in American bookstores a major section called 'self' in addition to the categories we have in Britain like 'sport', 'hobbies', 'romance', and so on. In this section is to be found paperback after paperback telling you how to run your life and how to resolve your problems. They are always written by psychologists or psychotherapists, the gurus who now provide directions for living. Bookshops without sections on 'religion' or 'sociology' have a section on 'psychology'.)

The answer given by the new gurus to those suffering or fearing the loneliness and confusion resulting from detaching themselves from a stable social order was that they could find direction for their lives by considering and following their inner needs. The goal is the self-actualized person. 'Such people become far more self-sufficient and self-contained. The determinants which govern them are now primarily inner ones, rather than social or environmental,'[3] says Abraham Maslow, one of the gurus of the movement. They were told that society was not, as it had been in all previous times, the provider of values and a force to be reckoned with, but the individual's handmaid in his or her quest for self-fulfilment.

In the 1950s and 1960s, more people migrated into California than into any other American state. People had been moving westward in search of the American dream for a hundred years or more, and California was the end of the trail for many. They could go no further west. And what did they find? An affluence that did not always satisfy, and neurosis in abundance. The search for fulfilment had no more promised lands to latch on to, for this *was* the promised land. So the search went inward, and what the pop psychotherapists offered appealed because it was very much in the American tradition of self-improvement. Improving one's material position had gone as far as any reasonable person would want, so the new goal of psychological self-improvement was invented. The search for the promised land, so central to American life, could go on after all, except that now it was a search for an inner land.

Maslow, one of those who offered tickets to this psychological promised land, made clear that his newly discovered theory of human needs had as much to do with providing a morality as with offering therapy:

This great frontier of research is our most likely source of knowledge of the values intrinsic to human nature. Here lies the value system, the religion-surrogate, the idealism-satisfier, the normative philosophy of life that all human beings seem to need, to yearn for, and without which they become nasty and mean, vulgar and trivial.[4]

In a society where the old bases for values are suspect, and the abyss of meaninglessness, relativism and absurdity begins to open up, Maslow and his colleagues came up with a system of values they believed to be objective and discoverable by science: literally, science will save humanity. This is the fulfilment of Auguste Comte's dream of one hundred and fifty years ago of a positive society based on the teachings of a new high priesthood of scientists; and of the view of some more recent scientists and philosophers that only facts are meaningful. If values are to come from anywhere, they are to come from facts, the facts of human nature. Maslow proclaimed he was committed to

attempt to do what the formal religions have tried to do and failed to do, that is, to offer people an understanding of human nature . . . a frame of reference in which they could understand when they ought to feel guilty and when they ought not to feel guilty . . . That is to say, we are working up what amounts to a scientific ethics.[5]

Science, not God or society, now provides human beings with values.

Maslow believed he had discovered that the lives of all human beings are governed by a hierarchy of basic needs. A need can be satisfied only when those lower in the hierarchy have first been met. Maslow's hierarchy is, from bottom to top: life, safety/security, belongingness/affection, respect/self-respect, self-actualization.

For those who had climbed up the ladder of American capitalism and still not found peace of mind, here was another ladder they could scale. Americans are preoccupied with achievement, yet their competitive economy means that only a few can actually get to the top; most are doomed by the system to achieving less than they had hoped for, as nine middle-aged executives out of ten know; and marriages rarely achieve the hopes of the romantic Hollywood image. Maslow provided something to strive for that everyone *could* achieve; if not to the top of the psychological hierarchy, at least a step or two further up. Unlike the pessimistic psychology of Freud in which the individual is doomed to internal strife, this new humanistic psychology is optimistic. People *can* do something about their situation; it is no use the person crying over his past, forever plagued by childhood traumas; and society is there as handmaid. This image of the self is thoroughly American and capitalist and individualistic. It directly mirrors what the immigrant just off the boat at New York felt in 1900: hopeful of at last being able to control his own destiny. The American dream dressed up in psychological garb.

This was a strange cure for isolation and loneliness. By asking the patient to gain direction from his or her own needs, by appealing to a whole gamut of values drawn from achievement-orientated, individualist capitalism, this therapy draws the individual yet further from society! As one researcher into American attitudes at the end of the 1970s found:

Among the people I interviewed, many truly committed self-fulfilment seekers focus so sharply on their own needs that instead of achieving the more intimate relationships they desire, they grow farther apart from others. In dwelling on their own needs, they discover that the inner journey brings loneliness and depression.[6]

Since this state is so similar to the original malaise, the

solution is clear to many: go for another course of psychotherapy, buy some more psychological self-help paperbacks. Like the consumer society that thrives on the needs that it itself helps generate, so too with the psychotherapy society.

With Maslow are founders of other schools of growth psychology, notably Carl Rogers and Erich Fromm. I have discussed Maslow, not because he is necessarily typical of growth psychology but because he has been particularly influential with a wider public. His work is very popular precisely because the model of the human personality, that he so clearly articulates, fits perfectly the emerging twentieth-century experience of needs. In a nutshell, needs are to be welcomed and the progressive meeting of them is just that — a mark of progress. He is also significant because he saw clearly that this version of needs is novel, historically unprecedented and goes against traditional Christian teachings; he was perhaps a little slow, however, in realizing how quickly the tide was turning in his favour.

Growth psychology's analysis of the origin of aggression is also revealing. Aggression is believed not to be an inborn instinct, but the result of the young infant's basic needs being frustrated (which happens to all infants to a greater or lesser extent). Thus, *the* original sin is to fail to meet a need. Now, it may be possible to integrate this theory with a Christian view as Claire Disbrey has recently suggested,[7] but my point is that growth psychology sees the failure to meet an infant's needs as inherently immoral: need is a moral, religious concept, not a neutral one.

**Psychology and Growth Psychology**
Some caveats. First, not all psychology holds this view of needs. Many psychologists think Maslow and Fromm, and still more their popularizers, to be bad psychologists because they introduce all kinds of metaphysical ideas into what should be an objective science. The critics claim that psychology should stick to observable behaviour, and they remind us that unobservable entities like 'self-actualization' or 'basic needs' are simply more or less helpful notions; they can never be proved to exist.

Far be it from me to get entangled in the civil wars of psychologists.[8] Such wars are crucial for the health of any discipline, but it is not for outsiders to become mercenaries in them. I merely wish to show how growth psychology has attained a mass popularity probably unmatched by any other brand of psychology. This is not to say that it is any truer, but that it fits the spirit of the age better than its rivals. And more than its rivals, it has articulated and influenced that spirit.

Secondly, there are versions of humanistic psychology that do not focus on the individual's need. In Viktor Frankl's logotherapy, for example, meaning is located *outside* rather than inside the individual. Further, some needs cannot become aims, and preoccupation with them is self-defeating:

The true meaning of life is to be found in the world rather than within man or his own psyche, as though it were a closed system . . . The real aim of human existence cannot be found in what is called self-actualisation. Human existence is essentially self-transcendence rather than self-actualisation. Self-actualisation is not a possible aim at all; for the simple reason that the more a man would strive for it, the more he would miss it . . . self-actualisation cannot be attained if it is made an end in itself, but only as a side-effect of self-transcendence.[9]

Self-actualization may be a desirable state but, like happiness, it is neither a need nor a goal (growth psychology oscillates between seeing it as each in turn), but a by-product. Frankl criticizes not self-actualization itself, but its being considered a need and placed within a framework that makes the individual focus on his own (or even others') needs.

Thirdly, growth psychology has to some extent provided a useful counterbalance to the apparent pessimism of Freudianism, and also to the nihilism and determinism of behaviourist psychology which often considers human behaviour to be as manipulable as that of rats. Freudianism makes clear that analysis is hard work and may reveal traumatic events in the past life of the patient that he or she can do little about, while behaviourism tends to be used by experts doing things *to* you. By contrast, there is a certain optimism in humanistic psychology; it tells the person that they can do something about their own situation, and at considerably less expense than a course of Freudian psychoanalysis.

**Economic Growth and Psychological Growth**

The parallels between psychological needs and economic needs are striking. Before elaborating, I want to emphasize that I am not trying to reduce one to the other. I am not saying that our economy results from the personal needs of individuals, nor that a certain view of psychology is determined by the economic relations of society, though there may be an element of truth in both those statements. Rather, both economic and psychological needs are part of a way of experiencing that is more deeply rooted in twentieth-century Western culture than simply the personality or the economy.

Firstly, growth psychology directly mirrors a growth economy. It is economic heresy to suggest, as some environmentalists have done, that perpetual growth is not a viable long-term goal because of the inevitable exhaustion of natural resources and that we should gear ourselves to a no-growth or steady economy. All governments today believe that their economies must be ever-expanding or else they will collapse. (This is partly fuelled by an economic cold war in which both West and East view the expanding economies of the other and feel they must either catch up or maintain their lead.)

Likewise growth psychology. A person either grows emotionally or stagnates. According to Maslow, you are motivated by the goal of meeting the particular need most dominant in your life, and when that is met you then become preoccupied with the next need up the hierarchy. Only when you have your need for physical safety and security satisfied do you crave affection; only when you feel loved do you become concerned with being respected; and so on. The person who has one need met and then does not move on to be concerned about higher needs will not fulfil him or herself — which is not to say that only those who get to the top of the hierarchy will be fulfilled, but that there must be a perpetual struggle upwards and that, utimately, the universe is on your side in this struggle. It is no more in the nature of the human personality to give up expansion of its own needs than it is in the nature of economies. Both kinds of expansion are seen as natural and good.

Just as the economist does not ask how material needs arise, but treats them as independent variables, so Maslow treats emotional needs. And like the economists, he does not ask what needs are *for.* To the psychologist, the only purpose in meeting one need seems to be to discover another, while to the individual each need appears as a goal, an end rather than a means. The final need, self-actualization, is described by Maslow as though it were not necessary *for* anything but as a goal, an end in itself. As with economics, so with psychology: failing to ask where needs come from and what they are for, implies that needs are natural, uncreated, given, inevitable and, therefore, good, right and proper.

Secondly, growth psychology not only mirrors an economy that creates needs, it also justifies it. In terms far more sophisticated than those of the television commercial, it informs us in the respectable name of science that needs are good and natural. People may be able to see through the commercial's claim that we need Daz or Crest, but on the psychotherapist's couch or reading the pop books on self, it is difficult to deny that one really needs affection, identity or whatever, that one really is a bundle of needs. We let our lives become far more dominated by such needs than ever we would be dominated by laundry powder or toothpaste. But, by making the language of needs intellectually respectable, growth psychology has actually made us more susceptible to material needs that are appealed to in cruder terms. If the television commercial implicitly appeals to our deeper psychological needs, then surely our resistance is lowered?

**Growth Psychology and Socialism**
That growth psychology is not a simple reflection of a capitalist economy but is far more deeply rooted is shown by its eager adoption by the New Left that has been so critical of capitalism; political radicals Herbert Marcuse and Christian Bay have drawn heavily on Fromm and Maslow respectively.

Growth psychology states that science must be committed to human well-being; 'it accepts the search for values as one of the essential and feasible tasks of a science of society' (Maslow). It provides criteria for what count as the real needs that a socialist society would be devoted to meeting, in contrast to the artificial and arbitary needs generated by capitalism. It provides an apparently scientific basis for politics. For Fromm, the sane society corresponds to the needs of man, not necessarily to what he feels to be his needs—because even the most pathological aims can be felt subjectively as that which the person wants most—but to what his needs are objectively, as they can be ascertained by the study of man.[10]

There has to be collaboration between social science and a radical politics to determine people's real needs and to create a society in which they can recognize them. For Marcuse,

In the last analysis the question of what are true and false needs must be answered by the individuals themselves, but only in the last analysis; that is, if and when they are free to give their own answer. As long as they are kept incapable of being autonomous, as long as they are manipulated . . . their answer to this question cannot be taken as their own.[11]

Until then, presumably, people's needs must be looked after by a paternalist Leninist government or the capitalist advertisers. Among all the talk (from business, from growth psychology, and from the New Left) of people discovering and knowing their own needs, in practice the expert (the advertiser, the psychologist, the political radical) always knows better than the masses what their needs are. This problem is inherent in the concept of need and will be returned to later.

It is easy for political and philosophical debates on need to get trapped in conventional political stereotypes. I do not wish this to happen in this book; I am as critical of the needs generated by Coca-Cola as of those generated by Herbert Marcuse. Need is far more deeply rooted in twentieth-century culture than much political debate assumes, much deeper than any simple left—right demarcation. And nothing shows this more clearly than growth psychology, for it is adopted in radical caucuses at the same time as it is spoken of in the board rooms of multi-nationals.

In the next three chapters, I want to show how a similar view of need is widespread not just in systems of thought like economics or psychology, but in our daily experience of work, sex, marriage and children.

# 5: Need in Work and Leisure

Why do people still want to consume when all their basic material needs have been met? This question was considered in chapter 3. Related questions are, why do people want to work when work is brutish or boring? Why do they want work when there is no work for them? Why do some people who do have jobs and whose jobs are neither brutish nor boring live for the weekends? In this chapter I want to explore the complex system of needs which govern work and play.

There are two main sorts of needs here:
1. The inner need to work, or the work ethic, which says that work is man's end in life, and that leisure is but a means to this end and should be minimized. The worker should take time off for only as long as is necessary to restore his body and spirit to work again.
2. The leisure ethic: leisure is the arena where all meaningful life takes place. Work is a means to provide leisure, and so the good life is one in which you work as little as possible.

Much of the confusion about work today results from the simultaneous presence in our lives of both these contradictory ethics.

### Toward the Work Ethic

Many ancient Greeks did not believe in work. Citizens did not work, but were supported by non-citizens (slaves and women) who toiled. The purpose of their work was to enable the citizen class to conduct the public life of politics, art and philosophy. Work was banished to the private sphere of the household, and was as invisible as in any totally automated scenario for the year 2100 AD. Citizens did not 'need' leisure, any more than slaves 'needed' work; leisure and work were simply the facts of life for each class respectively.

The Middle Ages saw a different view. For most people, work was morally neutral; it was simply what you had to do if you were going to clothe and feed yourself, and that applied to virtually everyone other than babes in arms. The highest calling, for the few, was not the life of a philosopher but a religious life. And for the many, work stopped on scores of days each year, the various saints' days and festivals; the Church's call to pray was more important than any need to work. Most people were happy with this; there was no inner compulsion to work more than was essential for providing the necessities of life and, in a farming community where work was uneven according to season and weather, little excuse was required to take days off and have a celebration.

Much has been written about how the seventeenth-century Puritans changed all this. Suffice it to say that they attempted to abolish the distinction between the secular work life of the many and the sacred religious calling of the few. For the Puritans, all work was to serve the community and to be done as to the Lord. All work could be consecrated to God, however mundane. This gave the ordinary believer a status comparable with the minister, at least in the more democratic Puritan sects, and it helped put an end to the medieval social order in which priest and people belonged to utterly separate social estates.

This was not work as an inner psychological need of the individual as we know it today. The focus was not the individual at all, but firstly God and then the community. The individual had an inner compulsion to work, but the compulsion came not from his own needs but from his God. The last thing the Puritans wanted was for a person to be driven by his inner needs. Work as a need, and work as a calling, are not the same thing at all. If a person did not want to work in Puritan days, he was denying not his own needs but the Creator who had called him to work. Nor did the Puritans necessarily identify work with paid employment; the wife sewing at home was as busy in the sight of her Lord as her husband in his employment. But among all these aspects of the Puritan view of work, most of which have disappeared now, there was one which was utterly crucial for the modern experience of work. Whether the Puritans invented it is debatable, but they were certainly the first to articulate it clearly: *work is important,* in more than the obvious sense that without it we die.

Then came the industrial revolution. At first this did not involve any great change in patterns of work. In the Lancashire cotton industry throughout the eighteenth century most work was put out to individual cottagers; they arranged their own hours, used the labour of the whole family, and made no distinction between work and family life.

A big change came with the move of production into factories. For the first time, it became important for production that workers clocked in and out at specified times, which was a strange notion to most because they went by the sun, or by the cries of the baby for food. Work in the factory was unpleasant. (Work at home had been equally unpleasant, but at least you were on home territory and therefore could organize your own day.) So the problem arose: how to get the masses into the factories, let alone get them there on time?

Well, better wages than could be obtained at home were the obvious answer, but alongside this came the ethic that work — in the form of paid employment, wage labour — is a good thing. 'Thou shalt work,' was the command, to which the reply is obviously, 'Says who?' 'God says,' sounded a lot better than, 'The boss says'. Build the workers chapels, preach them this ethic, and you should have little trouble from them. (Unfortunately, the chapels could not help but also teach them to read and tell them a little bit of God's justice, which in due course backfired on the employers in the form of nonconformist socialism.)

The Victorians soon added an important rider to the command: 'Thou shalt work' did not apply to women and children. Actually women and children continued to work, but the ideal put forward by moral reformers was that the man should go out to work to support his family. The wife should be at home having babies, frugally sewing and making jam, and the children should be at school learning to be good Christians and good seamstresses or good factory fodder. Increasingly, the labour at home of the middle-class wife, even when valued and appreciated, was not seen as work at all; work was what the man did when he went off to office or factory. So were introduced two important components of the industrial work ethic: that work equals paid employment; that it is men, not women, who need paid employment. There were now two classes of employees: the men who worked, because it was in their nature; and the women who worked, because unfortunately they had to or, in the eyes of many men, because they perversely wanted some money of their own.

As the comparative earning power of the woman was less than the man's, his need to work became doubly urgent. Practically, he *did* need to work long hours if he was to earn enough to keep his wife and family, for they could no longer keep themselves (in contrast to the medieval or peasant household in which women and children were not seen as dependents but as joint labourers). This then became part of his identity as a man: he needed employment if he was to see himself, and be seen by his wife, as a real man. This meant that a man could work long hours, hardly seeing his family and becoming virtually a stranger in the household, yet feel that what he was doing was very manly and very husbandly. A booming economy sometimes requires people to over-work in a way that conflicts with family life; to resolve this conflict, it is very convenient to have to hand an ideology that persuades the worker that what he is doing is actually supporting his family and enhancing his position within it.

This is the employment ethic more or less as we have inherited it today. What is remarkable about most employment today is not how boring or alienating it is, but how workers invest intrinsically boring and meaningless work with meaning. Their identity is so bound up with their role as workers that they make sure they convince themselves that their work is worthwhile — if not intrinsically, then for the money, the perks, or the comradeship. Many who have spent a lifetime in dirty, dangerous and ill-paid work dread retirement, and when they do retire often do not know what to do. Work is life.

Women too, are now claiming the paid employment ethic for themselves. Many far from destitute women have decided that their life in the home is even more of a prison than the husband's at work, and that they need paid employment if they are to maintain their personalities intact, and some say this in the name of women's liberation. Wages mean power.

Some, however, understand that the long-term goal of women in paid employment is not to gain worth from lousy jobs, like men do, but to redeem the dehumanized, depersonalized thing into which men have made work. It is women who can topple the notion that a person's worth derives from his or her work (a crazy notion when you consider that it is applied equally to the social worker and to the armaments manufacturer).

But generally the paid-employment ethic goes unchallenged. Particularly in the United States, the notion is still very much alive that vacations should be the bare minimum required to prevent the worker from having a nervous breakdown. In many companies, more than this bare minimum is not a right but a reward for loyal service over the years to the firm: the only thing that can possibly validate leisure, in this system, is work and commitment to the work ethic. Leisure derives from work, and is its servant.

### Toward the Leisure Ethic
Though the employment ethic is rarely challenged directly, it now has to co-exist with its polar opposite — a leisure ethic. How has this come about?

In order to keep working, people do need breaks and vacations. This is true not only of those whose work is physically heavy, but also of executives under mental and emotional stress. As one leading advocate of establishing a national system of wilderness areas in the United States argued:

In a civilisation which requires most lives to be passed amid inordinate dissonance, pressure and intrusion, the chance of retiring now and then to the quietude and privacy of sylvan haunts becomes for some people a psychic necessity. It is only the possibility of convalescing in the wilderness which saves them from being destroyed by the terrible neural tension of modern existence.[1]

What do people need vacations for? To keep them in good shape for work, is the answer of the work ethic. But as with all needs there is a tendency for the purpose to be lost sight of, and for the need to become an end in itself. In this case leisure becomes the main goal. Another American advocate of outdoor recreation seems to use need in this sense:

In a time of service industries, when most people make a living by selling things to one another or have jobs in which they are faceless components of superhuman organizations, recreation may represent the only chance many have to find themselves as unique individuals. Under these circumstances, recreation becomes a human need and must be recognised as a human right in the same sense that we have recognised needs and rights to health, education, and welfare.[2]

Here there is explicit recognition of the historical creation of recreation as a need. Whether this need is a means (necessary *for* something else), or an end (a 'human need'), is unclear; the need for leisure is rather like one of those ambiguous pictures in which you cannot decide which is figure and which is ground. Which is the basic ground of our existence, work or play? The answer depends entirely on whether you view play through the lens of the work ethic or the leisure ethic.

Given the less than totally satisfying nature of most employment, it is hardly surprising that many people come to see their work as simply a way of procuring the means to enjoy the good life in the spheres of family and leisure. This could mean one of two things. Either, that you minimize employment to the amount required to produce the necessities of life, leaving as much time as possible for the important things: making love, playing football, painting, writing books, evangelizing the unconverted, doing good works, or whatever. This is somewhat like the ancient Greeks, and has been revived recently by the hippies.

Or, and this is far more likely, you get caught in the trap that, in our society, most leisure activities cost money, considerable amounts of money. It is not cheap to take yourself, still less your family, off to the wilderness areas of the far West in the United States, to go sailing, or out for a nice meal, and most hobbies involve fancier and fancier gear. Nor is investing all in your home nest cheap either, as increasing numbers of comforts and gadgets become available: hot tubs, video recorders, and so on. So you want to maximize your leisure and family time, but you need to work long hours in order to be able to afford leisure and family time. You have to both work hard and play hard if you are to get the best out of life. Citizens of the United States are particularly keen on attempting this high pressure solution.

The hippy solution really goes against the capitalist grain. For once an economy has developed enough to provide the basic necessities of life, it is crucial that people expand their nesting, family and leisure consumption if the production of goods and services is to expand. To find ways of nesting and playing that do not cost money is a sure recipe for a no-growth economy, which as we have already seen is economic heresy. Unlike the other one, the hippy solution is always struggling against a system that ensures that as many of the good things of life as possible *do* cost money, a system that tells people that if they are to be human, if they are to love, if they are to be good to their spouses, if they are to give their children a good start in life, then they must consume.

Though the hippy solution is ill-fitted to a booming, fully employed capitalism, it may come into its own now that the spectre of automation looms ahead. Not that machines replacing labour are a new phenomenon, but in the past human beings were always needed to tend the machines. With automation, however, machines are tended by other machines. In industrial economies up to now, capital and labour needed each other. In boom time, employers needed as many workers as they could get, and workers always needed as much work as they could get. Both wanted to maximize work, and a work ethic suited both parties. But with automation, capital no longer needs labour, and labour is devalued. People talk of taking a pride in their work less than they did a couple of generations ago. So now both capital and labour want to minimize work; it has ceased to be a good and is now a necessary evil. If people continue to believe in a work ethic, or in the American work-plus-leisure ethic, then an automated worJd will be an unhappy world. A leisure ethic of the hippy variety certainly seems more suited to automation. Automation plus a hippy leisure ethic would not be so different from the aristocratic ethos of ancient Greece in which citizens led the good life of art and philosophy supported by a class of non-human workers, except this time the non-human workers are machines rather than women and slaves.

## Unemployment

Unemployment has become a fact of life for the 1980s. How it is experienced depends very largely on whether it is seen through the lens of the paid-employment ethic or the lens of the leisure ethic.

The employment ethic view of unemployment is the official view, and the view of most of those in work. It believes that unemployment is a spiritual disaster for a man; he virtually loses his soul. In past decades, when work was freely available, people just got on with their work and it was only a few social scientists who argued that men's work was part of their sexual identity and crucial for their self-respect. Now the unemployed person is inundated with official pamphlets which describe the various stages of trauma that he will go through, in the kindly hope that it will help him to know that his feelings of depression and desolation are shared by millions of others. The assumption is that most men do not realize how dependent on work they have become, and that they will need help in facing up to the bereavement of losing their job. Every television programme on unemployment likewise documents the devastating effect of unemployment on people's personal lives. (That the powers-that-be are also asking for voluntary redundancy is a bit awkward for them; on the one hand they are reinforcing the notion that unemployment is an unmitigated disaster, and at the same time asking for voluntary lambs to the slaughter.) What the effect of all this men-need-work talk is on those who still have work is unclear; whereas in the past they took their jobs for granted, now perhaps they feel they are psychologically dependent on a job, which considerably increases their exploitability.

Of course, all this rhetoric is applied only to men. Women work, it is officially held, not because they have any inner or emotional need to, but because they want the pin money. Therefore, if there is a choice, women should be fired before men, because they don't really need paid work. Most women workers would disagree with this, especially those about to be fired.

Nor is all this just talk. Many, many unemployed people—and especially unemployed men in their middle years—*do* feel shattered, useless, unable to cope. Over the course of two centuries, men have come to need work and to believe this need to be natural and proper. Those brought up to believe that work is life have few inner resources to cope with long-term unemployment.

Yet, there is growing evidence that the leisure ethic is enabling thousands of the unemployed to view unemployment positively. Thousands *do* take early retirement and voluntary redundancy. For them, work had always been a necessary evil that gave them the wherewithal to garden, paint, tinker with their motor cars, or whatever their passion in life was. A generous golden handshake enables them to spend *all* their time in the garden or under the car, and is welcomed. Others had always wanted to make a living out of their hobby, but never had the capital to get going, which is exactly what a redundancy payment or a handsome pension can provide.

When I was first unemployed in 1975, I welcomed the opportunity to do some research and writing that I knew no one would pay me for and that previously I had had to do in my spare time. I felt a sense of liberation now that the constraints of my old job as a university researcher were gone and I could now write about what I wanted, rather than what the research councils deemed to be socially necessary research. Immediately, people began to find my writing far more relevant and important, and I could see the absurdity of a system that, by letting committees decide what counts as relevant research, ended up funding spectacularly irrelevant research. It was in fact this period of creative unemployment that gave me the courage to become a self-employed writer, and so my hobby became my life. Little do the authorities realize how productive were those few hundred pounds of unemployment benefit in comparison to the thousands of research-fund pounds they had previously lavished on me!

Without denying my own experience, people told me that I was an exception: few had a creative and cheap hobby like writing, and few could afford to approach unemployment in this aristocratic/Greek style. For millions, unemployment was a disaster. Well, indeed it was, and is, but there is growing evidence that the masses of young unemployed do not see it as unmitigated disaster, and that they are developing a new leisure ethic all their own, uninfluenced by either hippiedom or ancient Greece. Liverpool sociologist Ken Roberts[3] has interviewed unemployed young people and found them considerably happier with their lot than the conventional wisdom will allow. They certainly prefer unemployment to the various slave-labour schemes run by the government which get young people to work a forty-hour week for no more than dole money. Seen as solutions to the problem of youth unemployment by the authorities, these schemes are often experienced by the young people themselves not as the solution but as the problem. Unemployment, like divorce, is difficult when it is a rarity; you feel an outcast, nobody respects you, you have no money when standards of consumption are set by the majority who have, and you despise yourself. But when most of the young people in your town are unemployed, then you are no longer a freak. You are normal; you have grown up to expect this; it is life; and you cannot understand those adults who cannot understand why you do not find it a problem.

Surely there is a tremendous resource here that could be developed, an embryonic ethic that will enable people to respond positively to unemployment and automation.[4] But instead it is abhorred by the powers-that-be. The respectable middle aged who are employed, or those whose husbands are employed, comment with disdain how youngsters today do not really want to work; there is plenty of work they believe, it's just that kids aren't bothered to look. Well, they are wrong that there is plenty of work, but they may be right that the kids aren't bothered. But what do they want, these moral guardians of the old order? In a society which does not have jobs for everyone, surely it is better that the minority that can't work is the minority that doesn't want to work? Given how many do want to work, it makes sense to grant the wishes of those who do not.

But instead the system hounds them. I recall being interviewed back in 1978 by an unemployment review officer who was pressing me as to why I had not yet found a job, and I tried putting such points to him. Why did he want me to take a job, any job? Why did he want me, who was quite happy unemployed, to take a job for which I was grossly overqualified and which would bore me to tears, when this would undoubtedly condemn someone else who desperately needed that job to a life of misery on the dole queue? How could he, an official of the 'welfare' state, claim that this in any way aided anyone's welfare? Well, he admitted that he couldn't, but rules were rules, and they stated that after a certain period of time social security officials had to press the unemployed to take any job going, however unsuited for them.

The old employment ethic is so insecure, so inappropriate today, that its guardians become ever more rigid, venting their anger on those who challenge them. As one unemployed British kid commented in 1982:

They're sympathetic as long as you are portraying the right image of an unemployed person — and that is uptight, depressed, miserable

57

and guilty. If you happen one day . . . to decide to put a defiant smile on your face, it's not my fault and why should I waste every minute of the day going insane over it, then they begin to doubt that you really care; and not to care about being unemployed is forbidden because that puts you on equal footing with them.[5]

Perhaps there is some hope of change. That quote was from the BBC's *Radio Times,* hardly a seedbed of radical fervour. That such a dissident voice was allowed to appear there suggests that the absurdity of an unmodified employment ethic is becoming apparent even to the official voice of reason. What is certain, though, is that the current bout of unemployment is bringing to the surface both the work ethic and the leisure ethic. Hitherto largely implicit, they are now articulated in all shapes and sizes. Indeed, it is impossible to talk of the social consequences of unemployment without reference to one or the other or both. And it is because they are so fundamentally opposed to each other that there are such divergent experiences of unemployment. As indeed there always have been of retirement: some begin to flourish in retirement as at long last they begin to live, without the millstone of toil around their necks; others don't know what to do with themselves and die within the year, leaving behind a widow who for the next twenty years consoles herself with the knowledge that, without work, her man would not have been happy anyway.

Diametrically opposed though they be, both work and leisure ethics are in tune with the times, for both are based on need. Men need to work, says the work ethic. Recreation is a human need says the leisure ethic. The two actually feed off each other. On the one hand, an unbalanced world of work has generated such pressures that individuals either need recreation to recuperate, or they have become so turned off work that they live for the hours when they are not working. And on the other hand, the high cost of consuming means we have to work to earn the cash to pay for our leisure.

Surely, these needs are not healthy. As they are manifested in our society, the need for leisure and the gross need for paid work are not needs that should be met; they should be abolished. The key is the provision of satisfying work that does not generate needs that have to be met through consumption. We have to break the vicious circle in which the more unfulfilling paid work is the more people need it! Once broken, there would then be no need for perpetual growth in the industrialized world, clearly unsustainable in the long run, and resources could be diverted to the poor of the world — without loss to the rich nations because they would no longer need the resources. For the rich nations, work and play would be redeemed. No longer needs, they could be enjoyed for the positive things that they undoubtedly are.

# 6: The Needs of the Sexes

In previous chapters I have shown how paid employment, consumption beyond subsistence, leisure as a separate time from work, and psychotherapy, are maintained by the generation of personal needs. What about sex and marriage? On investigation we find that they too are generally described today as governed by a similar system of mutual needs. 'I love you' is often translated today as 'I need you'. This is rather curious, for love is total giving of self to another, whereas need is the using of the other for one's own purposes. How can the two words be used interchangeably? How can love use the other to meet one's needs? What are these needs?

There are several ways in which the needs of women and men interlock. To illustrate this, I describe in this chapter one form of marriage. I do not claim all marriages to be of this particular kind.

### Men's Needs

This first need of most men in our society is practical. They have not been taught how to cook and mend and sew. There is no reason why boys are unable to learn these things, but generally they are not taught, for it is assumed they will marry and their wives will do these things for them. If they have been rendered unable to look after themselves, this is a very good reason why they do indeed need a wife. A friend of mine described his falling in love and getting married as 'finding the woman who will look after me for the rest of my life'. There have been some token changes of late in what boys are taught, but both their formal education at school and their informal education at home are still grossly lacking in the basic skills of looking after oneself, and all studies show that in marriage the vast majority of basic tasks are still done by the wife. There is much talk of change, but rather little actual change.

Secondly, it is commonly assumed that one reason for marriage or co-habitation is the man's biological need for regular sex. Certainly St Paul granted this as a valid reason for marriage. Recently, however, the Hite report survey of seven thousand American males has questioned this.[1] Although men assume that they are biologically driven to have sex, Ms Hite observes: 'If I was a man I would rather think that I had choices than that I was biologically driven, but many men hate the idea.' Why? The one clear advantage of believing themselves biologically driven when in fact they have choices is that they are abrogated of responsibility for their actions—which is what has excused men since time immemorial for anything from rape to insensitivity to their wife's feelings. (The notion that some people are *homo*sexually driven by their hormones and that this too justifies their behaviour is equally dubious and equally often resorted to nowadays.)

If their hormones do not instruct them to have intercourse, why are men so keen on it? Ms Hite continues:

The stereotype was that men want intercourse because that provides their best orgasm. So I asked men why do you want intercourse? They replied, not for the orgasm because I can have a stronger orgasm physically during masturbation. That for me instantly cuts across the idea that intercourse is demanded by a male sex drive. They gave me three reasons why they want intercourse—because there was a complete body closeness at that time, which is what women also said when asked why they liked intercourse; because they felt free to be out of control, as out of control as their wives. You're still manly if you are out of control during intercourse, but not at other times. The third reason was because if you are not having regular intercourse you are not a man . . .

The answer to why men want sex so much is that they are trying to make physical sex a substitute for verbal closeness. They have been brought up to feel ridiculous sort of mushing over their feelings—that's soap opera stuff, for women. But it's okay to do all that during sex.[2]

This explanation may or may not be correct, but it certainly does fit with something that is generally agreed, that most men have difficulty expressing weakness and emotion, or at least those of Anglo-Saxon stock do. Boys are taught to put a brave face on things and not to cry; it is thought unmanly to express tenderness. Girls, by contrast, are encouraged to cry and giggle, and even to invent feelings.

Whereas vulnerability in a woman may enhance her sexual

attractiveness, it is thought to detract from a man's. The taboo on men expressing feelings creates a third reason why they need sex and marriage: to find an outlet for their feelings. Our society has declared romance, marriage and in particular the bed to be the one place where men can have a cuddle, admit they have needs, and admit that they feel fond of someone. Whereas women can express fondness and walk arm in arm with other women in public, there is a strict taboo on men doing this with anyone other than their lover or their children, and for some men anywhere other than in bed. That this is a taboo rather than a man's nature is shown by the many societies, such as the Latin countries, where men *are* allowed to display emotions in public.

This taboo on expressing feelings and fondness can make men lonely. If they cannot express feelings with anyone other than their lover, if they cannot display their weakness, then there are limits to how close they can get to anyone else. So the man, often more so than the woman, looks to marriage to cure his loneliness. He expects the woman to be a soul-mate, someone with whom at last he can share everything. The tragedy is that, all too often, his curb on displaying any weakness is so powerful that he cannot even display it to his wife, and the loneliness becomes ever deeper as he dutifully enacts the role of the all-competent, all-knowing man-the-protector. Or his wife may expect him to play this role, and discourage expression of weakness.

This may have its origins in boyhood. Boys are brought up to have vulnerable egos. Their parents tell them that their role in life is the breadwinner and that their self-respect as a man depends on their role as worker, yet they are then thrust into a competitive capitalist economy in which, by definition, there are more losers than winners. For everyone with a prestigious job, there are ten with jobs that really do not amount to very much. Even those who have prestigious jobs fear the spectre of sickness, unemployment and retirement; if their job is what makes them who they are, then what will happen when the job comes to an end? Act Two of this drama starts with marriage, when the wife takes over from the man's parents. With such a shaky basis for his identity, the man needs his wife to boost his ego, which she faithfully does; she is grateful for the money he brings home, pathetically earned though it was; she maintains the charade that he is a wonderful lover; she applauds the miniscule amounts of time that he spends looking after the children. The man desperately needs this continual affirmation; many a man with a stressful or boring job has gladly admitted, 'If it wasn't for my wife, I couldn't keep going'.

So, men need wives and lovers to look after them, to cuddle, to befriend them, and to tell them what wonderful people they are. These needs have been socially created, and they are the reasons men get married and stay married (or co-habit); more particularly, they are the reasons why sex and marriage or having a lover is *so* important to them.

**Women's Needs**
With such a range of needs to cater for, what's in it for the woman? Well, she has a need which rather neatly dovetails with her man's need for her, for she believes that she needs to be needed. Though she may say that everyone has a need to be needed, it is striking that it is very largely women who talk of this need. Girls are brought up to see their task in life as servicing and caring for men and children.

This poses a bit of a problem nowadays. Caring for others means giving, and this ill fits the dominant notion that all human actions, or at least all worthwhile human actions, are motivated by need. Need focuses on the ego; giving focuses on the other. Today the usual way out of this puzzle is in terms of the need to give; in this way, self-giving and self-sacrifice can be seen as meeting the needs of the self, which does not threaten the way we like to see ourselves. What it means in marriage is that the woman is getting as much out of servicing the husband's needs as the man is. What might have been seen as exploitation of the woman is recast as the mutual meeting of need.

Even more than her husband, a woman's children need her. Not all husbands may be dependent on their wives in the way described, but certainly all young children are utterly dependent, and that dependence is largely on their mothers. If her husband does not make her feel needed, her babies do. Motherhood is like marriage in being based on mutual need: the child needs her mother, the mother needs to be needed, and so the mother needs her children.

Most likely, this will leave the woman alone at home much of the time looking after her children; if so, another need arises—to be financially supported. As ever, one need produces another. The woman must then rely on her knight-in-shining-armour, her man. This is the deal: 'I look after you for the rest of your life. You support me financially for the rest of my life.' The man is not only the better earner, as a result of inequality in employment, but he is also deemed to be the stronger and the more intelligent. So, not only is it in the man's interest that his vulnerable ego be boosted by his woman, but it is in hers that she really believes he is strong and intelligent and capable of bringing in a decent and secure income. His need and hers are mutually complementary.

To these needs—to be needed, for children and for financial support—may be added one more recent addition. The woman's need for sex. Men have always been considered to have a biological need for sex, but it is only recently that women have publicly announced that their own sexual lives may be seen in the same way. Contemporary surveys indicate that women enjoy not only intercourse or orgasm, but the whole range of touch and closeness and affection. But a preoccupation with orgasm became fashionable in the 1960s and early 1970s, a belief that orgasm is really what sex is all about, or should be about, and so orgasm became a need. If not met, then this was grounds for finding a new lover, or educating the old one, or joining a sex-therapy course, or somehow or other ensuring that this need was met. Thankfully, this phase seems now to be in decline, and people are perhaps less hung-up about sex than a decade ago.

But am I simply carping over phraseology? Women were discovering their sexuality and to call it a need was simply a particularly powerful way of expressing its goodness. Indeed, it is an excellent example of how any good thing today gets labelled 'a need'. It shows how need is one of the most persuasive moral words in our language.

## Who Needs Who, Really?
If sex and marriage are experienced as a mutual meeting of need, how are these needs generated and maintained? Answers to this question hinge on the biological fact that it is women who bear children. This creates a basic inequality between man and woman, but who is the loser in this inequality?

One answer notes that women may or may not have some

emotional or biological need to produce children, but what is certain is that the human race—and in a male-dominated society, that means men—need women to produce children. This gives women enormous power; ultimately men need women more than women need men.

How then are men to have any control over women? One main tactic is for men to take control of the spheres of work and of politics, to discriminate against women in those spheres, to confine them to the private and therefore harmless arena of the home.

But the home is not such a harmless place. Not only do men need women to bear children, but they have also delegated to them the rearing of children, so that women have in their hands the formation of the personalities of both the men and the women of the next generation. She who rocks the cradle rules the world. She ensures that the boys grow up with vulnerable egos. She encourages the girls in their desire for babies, for therein lies real power. She creates an image of woman being the weaker partner, the one with 'needs', in order to create a smokescreen so that men do not see their lack of power, but rest impotently in the naive belief that, because they control work and politics, they actually run the human show. The only weakness in this programme is that girls as well as boys may come to believe that they really are the weaker sex, and therefore make themselves incapable of wielding the power that nature has given them.

The other answer notes that women's childbearing function makes them economically dependent on men for several years. In the past, most of a woman's adult life was spent bearing and nursing children, since women had more children and died younger than today. Over the millennia this has produced their general dependence on men; women need men more than men need women. What is to stop the man walking out of the marriage, leaving behind an unsupported wife and ten children? How is the woman to keep her man?

As the underdog, the woman has to learn to understand and manipulate personal relations. 'Feminine intuition is the insight of the underprivileged.'[3] It is no coincidence that most romances are written either by women or from the woman's point of view. Though economically dependent on her man, she manipulates his emotions so that he becomes emotionally dependent on her. While courting, she gives the impression of being more involved than she is. The man marries her, thinking he has her at his beck and call, but in fact she has got him to fall in love with her so that she has *him* grovelling at *her* feet. With no economic resources, she uses the politics of love to restore some measure of power to herself. She creates needs in her man which she leads him to believe only she can meet, while propagating an image of herself as the emotional one.

I remain agnostic as to which, if either, of these stories best accounts for the system of needs that marriage has become. I am neither psychologist nor political theorist. All I am concerned to document in this chapter are the following:

1. One particular way in which men's and women's needs can interlock in marriage. I would not claim that exactly the same needs are met in every marriage!

Indeed, in some sections of the population, marriage may not be experienced as a mutual meeting of needs at all. A study by sociologists Young and Willmott in the 1950s showed that among working-class couples from Bethnal Green in London's East End many of the women's needs were met by female kin.[4] At the other end of the social ladder, many royal and aristocratic mothers in Britain are needed in public engagements, and most of their babies' needs may be met by paid nannies rather than by the mother.

However, marriage as the mutual meeting of need is the romantic view held by most of the middle classes, among which we find women's magazine writers, romance novelists, social workers, magistrates, clergymen, marriage counsellors and the whole panoply of those professionally engaged in advising and forming our attitudes to sex, marriage and divorce. From their mouths and pens has come the received wisdom that marriage is the mutual meeting of personal need. In the more extreme romantic view, marriage is seen as the total meeting of *all* the emotional needs of each partner.

2. This is believed to be a good thing. It is in fact believed to be the moral basis of marriage, and it has become the criterion by which many people assess their marriages and love affairs. If I can no longer meet your needs, then that is a *prima facie* ground for your separating from me. You would be untrue to yourself and to your own needs were you to stay with me.

(You may remain because of the needs of the children. But there would be a conflict, as much moral as practical, between your needs and their needs. See chapter 7.)

3. Even some of the most ardent critics of the institution of marriage, notably some feminists, believe that sexual relations and living together (either heterosexually or homosexually) should be based on mutual need. The main criticism of marriage is not that it should be based on something other than mutual need, but that it does not meet the needs of the woman. Other ways of living closely with other human beings must be explored, in which everyone's needs *are* met. This supposedly radical criticism of marriage actually shares with the more usual romantic concept of love the assumption that meeting each other's needs is what human life is all about. Just as assumptions about need lie deeper than any left—right division, so they also transcend the rift between those who 'support' and those who 'attack' the family.

**Falling in Love**
Even though men and women are motivated by their needs to marry, lifelong commitment to another can still be a somewhat daunting prospect in a society that values freedom and personal autonomy. Many people require the ecstatic state of falling in love to propel themselves into a lifelong dependence on one person. They know that no one individual can meet all their needs, but in love they so desire the other person and long to give themselves to the other that their own needs recede into the background. For some, being in love may involve the feeling that already they need the other utterly; for some, it induces a neediness that had not been there before, a neediness the lover welcomes. Either way, being in love causes them to welcome a union in which they will grow to need each other—absolute mutual need, nirvana indeed.

Well, that's how being in love gets some people to the altar. But it doesn't always work. Being in love does heighten your dependence on the other, but rather than enabling you to accept that dependence, it may scare you off—especially if you are a man. For, according to the Hite report, men are often highly ambivalent about being dependent on others:

In the beginning, the descriptions [from men] of falling in love were similar to what women might say. Some of the real ecstatic feelings are the same, but many men very soon resented being in love, whereas women usually enjoyed being in love. They resented it because they felt out of control, and were in a woman's control. I think that explains why a lot of men after falling in love withdraw, leaving the woman wondering why, since he seemed to be as in love as she was. And most men didn't seem to be marrying the women they were most passionately in love with. They really felt uncomfortable in a situation in which they were very vulnerable.[5]

Also, falling in love may not be quite so mutual as at first appears. Dating has often aimed at getting the other to fall in love with you while you retain control of your own feelings. The rhetoric is romantic love, but the reality can be cynicism as you succeed in catching the boy or the girl that your peer group would approve of.[6]

Being in love, then, can successfully prepare lovers for a union of mutual need; or it can markedly mess things up, marrying you to someone you certainly do not need and perhaps do not even love, or propelling you into an exploitative relationship under the name of love.

Being in love, however, can also transcend the whole system of love as mutual need and open a higher way, as C. S. Lewis has brilliantly shown in *The Four Loves*. He distinguishes need-pleasures that focus on the individual who has the pleasure and what it does for him (the thirsty man's 'I needed that glass of water'), and appreciative-pleasures which focus on the object of pleasure (the connoisseur's 'That wine was marvellous'). Venus, or sexual desire, is a need-pleasure in which the other is a means to satisfying my desire; Eros, or being in love, is an appreciative pleasure in which I desire a woman for herself, not because she is a woman (for any woman can satisfy the need for sex). I do not desire her as a means for satisfying my sexual desire. Indeed, sexual desire is not paramount and may not come first in time.

Eros thus wonderfully transforms what is *par excellence* a Need-pleasure into the most Appreciative of all pleasures. It is the nature of a Need-pleasure to show us the object solely in relation to our need, even our momentary need. But in Eros, a Need, at its most intense, sees the object most intensely as a thing admirable in herself, important far beyond the lover's need.[7]

Not only do I not see the beloved in relation to my own needs, I do not see her in relation to her needs either. I do not see her as a bundle of needs which I can meet. Rather she is a unique and total person in whom I rejoice. Needs, hers or mine, simply do not come into it. We are dealing here with persons, not with needs. As Lewis notes, this is one of the few occasions when we find human beings loving in a way akin to the love of God as described in the Christian tradition (which incidentally may be why we are prone to idolize being in love).

Yet at the very moment that the experience of being in love begins to question the whole framework of love and marriage as a mutual meeting of need, the twentieth century comes lumbering back in with its language of need. Though the experience contradicts the framework of need, we often describe the experience through the framework's language. 'I need you, baby', 'I'd die without you', and so on. This is a good example of how the language of need neutralizes those experiences that have the potential to challenge it, and indeed even enlists them in its own army. Other examples will become apparent in due course.

# 7: Children's Needs

*Two year old:* 'I want to go potty.'
*Mother:* 'No. You *need* to go potty.'

In some phases of the Christian era, children have been seen as bundles of sin requiring discipline. They are full of desires and wants, most of which are intrinsically evil, out of which they must be wooed by Christian love or coerced by Christian teaching. This is why the 1662 Anglican Prayer Book exhorted that children 'be brought up in the fear and nurture of the Lord', and 'to the praise of his holy name'. For, if this was successful, the child had been rescued from the devil and another sinner had been saved for the kingdom. This view of the child affirme 1 the centrality of the Christian religion in people's lives.

Throughout human history, another view of children has been even more widespread, a view that affirmed the centrality in people's lives of the struggle for physical survival. Most children who have ever lived have ceased to be children around the age of four or five. They then became small adults. Once they had learnt to control their bowels, to talk, and to find their own way home from short distances, they were set to help the grown-ups. They did the same tasks as the adults, though with a much reduced workload and allowed to mix play in with their allotted tasks, in much the same way as today you may see the three- or four-year-old son of a farmer or farm labourer out with his dad, making hay, discussing whether the soil is too wet for planting, and occasionally stopping to throw stones into the pond or jump into a puddle. Most children, then, have been seen as mini-workers, contributing to the family economy; the puberty rites that many tribes conduct mark not the transition from childhood as we know it to adulthood, but from this status of mini-adult to full member of the tribe.

## Inventing Childhood
Not so today. Between infancy and adolescence is a prolonged and supposedly idyllic status called childhood. This is marked by three things: play rather than work, being at school instead

of in employment, and a particularly close and affectionate relationship with the parents, especially with the mother. All three features are innovations. The child is seen neither as a bundle of sin nor as a small worker, and the way is opened up for the child to be seen instead as a bundle of needs.

In the early nineteenth century, children became a public issue, as reformers and philanthropists became concerned about their exploitation in the factories. The exploitation, of course, derived from their being used as mini-workers; this was not so terrible in itself, but it was *all* they were allowed to be as they toiled for twelve hours each day in the factories. The reformers wanted them at home and in school, learning useful crafts and the Christian religion. They certainly did not want them to be idle, 'for the Devil makes use of idle hands', even little hands; but the belief was spreading that they were not little adults. They were something different, special: children.

Many of the Victorian reformers reinforced the Christian notion of children as bundles of sin—which was why they needed the moralizing influence of education and of their mothers rather than the brutalizing influence of the factory foreman. But soon Victorian romanticism joined forces with Victorian moralism, and there emerged the notion of the child as an angel of light. After all, this was the period that put the Wife and Mother on a pedestal, and surely such divine beings could not produce bundles of sin from their wombs? So the Child joined the Mother on the pedestal. Victorian painters began to paint children's faces like Rubens painted cherubim.

All this was undoubtedly beneficial for the children, for it *did* take them out of the factories; it did teach them to read and write; never again could respectable society be complacent about suffering children. Of course, not all children were that enamoured with their schoolmasters and marms, and not all middle-class children enjoyed being dressed up to look like cherubim. (This is one of my father's most vivid and distasteful memories from his early childhood at the end of the Victorian era.) But none would have chosen to go back to the factory or down the pit.

From the end of the First World War, an increasing number of mothers found themselves at home alone with their young children. The next few decades, with a peak in the 1950s, saw the drawing together of the Victorian ideals of the Wife/Mother and the Child into the dominant twentieth-century belief that children need their mothers. The psychologist John Bowlby wrote many things, but the one that was latched onto and repeated time and again was from a monograph for the World Health Organisation in 1951 in which he used the term 'maternal deprivation'. He was referring to gross loss by the child of the mother's presence (as in a case of prolonged hospitalization of the child), which could clearly be traumatic in a society where young children had no one other than their mother to look after them. But he was widely quoted in defence of the view that *any* departure of the mother from her child was bad for the child, and that the mother should therefore be with her child twenty-four hours a day. In the most extreme form of this paranoia, some women seriously began to wonder whether they dare leave their baby with grannie or a neighbour even for one hour, lest it be permanently damaged psychologically![1]

The child was idolized. The goddess Wife/Mother had become a priestess who sacrificed herself to the full-time service of this new god. Idolizing the child provided meaning for the family. While I was preparing this book, some friends understood broadly what it was about. They agreed that needs were socially constructed. But the one stumbling block, especially for women, was the children. 'Surely children's needs aren't constructed? Surely they are real? What do you want — a return to the exploited factory urchin?' Meeting their children's needs was something they dared not reconsider; to think that children might not need them was to think the unthinkable.

With the decline of religion, and the decline of first the British Empire and then of America's world dominance, we are not at all sure what we are living for. People had once seen child-rearing as a matter of imparting knowledge and values and standards to our children, but now we do not know what values we really believe in. But we do believe in romantic love and romantic parenthood, like country and western singer Don Williams who brings his bizarre list of disparate beliefs to a climax with, 'I believe in children . . . I believe in you.' This is 'child-centred parenthood'.[2] As Dr Benjamin Spock put it: 'The tendency is for American parents

to consider the child at least as important as themselves —
perhaps potentially more important.'[3]

Dr Mia Kellmer Pringle, one of Britain's leading child
experts, is convinced that

There are four basic emotional needs which have to be met from the
very beginning of life to enable a child to grow from helpless infancy
*to mature adulthood* [my emphasis]. These are: the need for love
and security; for new experience; for praise and recognition; and for
responsibility.

Yet what is 'mature adulthood'? Dr Pringle does not know
any more than do Britain's parents. One of her 'unanswered
questions' at the end of her book, *The Needs of Children,* is
'Into what kind of people do we want today's children to
grow?'[4] In a world where nothing seems certain, we latch
onto one thing that does seem certain: that children have
definite and identifiable needs. We can all agree that these
needs must be met if they are to grow up into decent human
beings, though as a society we haven't the faintest clue what
a decent human being is. Nor have most parents. We don't
know what these needs are needed *for*, but that they *are*
needed has become unquestionable dogma.

Even if we *were* agreed as to what sort of society we want,
and obviously there is some measure of agreement, what
children need would vary considerably from one society to
another. What children in the USSR and in the USA are
deemed by their parents to need is very different; the whole
pattern of child rearing is different, as Urie Bronfenbrenner
has shown in his fascinating study, *Two Worlds of
Childhood.*[5] Whether children need to become spontaneous,
competitive and happy as in America, or self-controlled, co-
operative and willing to defer gratification as in Russia, are
conclusions that differ enormously. For example, Russians
are passionately fond of children, but this fondness extends
to all children not just their own; it would be thought very
strange for pre-school children to spend most of their time
with their own mothers. Even other children demonstrate
fondness for little ones. Bronfenbrenner recalls one incident
on a Moscow street:

Our youngest son—then four—was walking briskly a pace or two
ahead of us when from the opposite direction there came a company

of teenage boys. The first one no sooner spied Stevie than he opened his arms wide and, calling 'Ai malysh!' (Hey, little one!), scooped him up, hugged him, kissed him resoundingly, and passed him on to the rest of the company, who did likewise, and then began a merry children's dance, as they caressed him with words and gestures. Similar behaviour on the part of any American adolescent male would surely prompt his parents to consult a psychiatrist.

In the Russian system, children *need* this warmth and affection from everyone if they are to become secure, co-operative citizens. Contrast the clinging, possessive American who invests all in an exclusive love relation (with either child or spouse) as a haven from a heartless competitive world.

People in the West today talk as though their children's needs were universal, timeless. This clearly is not the case. What children need differs widely depending on their society's vision of the ideal citizen or human being. It is only by refusing to ask 'For *what* does the child need a close relation with its mother/new experiences/etc?', that we can kid ourselves that such needs are timeless. Just consider how rarely one hears today, compared with only a few decades ago, a father saying, 'What that child needs is a good thrashing!' and it becomes obvious that children's needs are *not* timeless.

In the absence of common values, child rearing has changed in the West from the imparting of values to the meeting of the children's needs. (Or so we seem to think; in fact one cannot but impart values to children.) I have said earlier that the contemporary experience of needs is part and parcel of a view in which human beings are alone in the universe and have nothing to focus on other than their own and each other's needs. This is particularly true of the modern family. Treating work mainly as a means of earning money for the family, disenchanted with politics, isolated from other relatives and possibly also from neighbours, Mum, Dad and the kids *are* alone in the little universe of their family.[6] What can be their reference point? For many, the answer is: the Child.

So what happens when this Child grows up? Such children are likely to face an identity problem. For if there was nothing outside of the family to live for, then what are they to live for when they leave home? One of two solutions is likely. If they have been the centre of their parents' universe, they may simply become spoiled and never really grow up, thinking themselves the centre of everyone else's universe. Of course, they will get a painful shock sooner or later, unless they are fortunate and find lovers who consider them the centre of *their* universe. Or a girl raised in this way may draw the conclusion not that she herself is the centre of the universe, but that children in general are. So she gets married and has children as soon as possible. (There is evidence that many girls see marriage as simply a means to motherhood.) One mother—a teacher who enjoyed her career—confided to me how she is at pains to tell her two daughters how much she loves them and how important they are to her. Yet she was dismayed when her ten-year-old informed her that she intended to get married and have children by the time she was twenty. The mother understood the problem: how could the daughter aspire to anything else if she was the apple of her mother's eye?

If mothers need their children so, it would be pretty traumatic for the mothers if their children did not need *them.* This is why it is cute to hear a two-year-old say, 'I need [rather than I want] to go potty'. The child's need stresses his status as child; it stresses his dependence on Mum. The child who always says 'I want' even if his wants are quite legitimate, like 'going potty', is definitely not approved of. In previous eras, we wanted to drill all wants and desires out of a child for they were by definition sinful; today we attempt to convert those wants into needs, to convert potential assertiveness into declarations of dependence.

Because there is no one else to look after them, many children *are* dependent on their mothers. This is what American commentators have called 'momism'. Doubtless being deprived of their mother for even brief periods *is* a problem for some children growing up in this kind of household. Certainly it becomes a problem for adolescents as they have to challenge Mum and Dad; and a problem for them too, for a rebellious teenager is like the centre of their universe exploding, a steady state sort of universe becomes a big-bang universe. And then there is a problem too for the mother when all the children have left, and her universe no longer has a centre.

## The End of the Child?

The era of the child may well prove to be short-lived historically, perhaps no more than a few generations. As early as 1941, Max Horkheimer noted that 'American children, far from becoming overly dependent on their mothers, form strong attachments to neither parent, acquiring instead, at an early stage in their lives, a cool, detached, and realistic outlook on the world.'[7] This is deeply distressing to parents brought up to believe in the Child. They cannot understand why children 'aren't like they used to be', 'they seem to miss out on childhood these days'. Six-year-olds are no longer innocent, but cynical, worldly wise. 'You can't teach them anything, these days. They know it all.' Not 'they *think* they know it all', for the parent realizes with a shock how much they *do* know!

One result of this is that adolescence is disappearing. Adolescence as a 'phase', as a problem, was created by the difficulty of transforming the innocent Child into a responsible adult. But those youngsters who never go through the Child phase find their teenage years remarkably trouble free, or remarkably so to their parents who were once children. Children are reverting to what, historically, they have always been — little adults.

The passing of the Child is deeply mourned by the older generation, who feel that the children of today are losing a lot by never having been through childhood. They look back longingly to their own childhood. Escapist, romantic coffee table books on Edwardian childhood abound in the shops; country and western superstar Dolly Parton sings lovingly of her childhood with Mom.

Why has the change happened? It seems most unnatural to the older generation, though historically it is a reversion to the normal, and perhaps does not require explanation. What does require explanation is the historical anomaly of the invention of the Child. Also, it may well be that most lower-class children never went through the era of the Child anyway; they were always out on the street, out of the influence of their parents, much to the disgust of the reformers who wanted to make them into Children.

What do today's children themselves feel? Are they aware they have lost anything? It seems not. Perhaps like slaves and blacks, whom their masters had thought were better off in their childlike dependence and for whom their masters feared when liberation enabled them to face the world without their masters' protection, children too have no regrets at losing much of their dependent status. Sure, life is harder for them (just like it was for many slaves thrust out into the harsh world of competitive capitalism) but, just like the slaves, children do not appear to want it any different. Perhaps it is the parents who are the main losers?

### 'For the Sake of the Children'

Despite signs of imminent and mysterious disappearance from Western civilization, the Child is still with us to no small extent. I have noted that the Child is most likely to become the centre of a family's universe when the family has no other centre. Marriage partners are least likely to have shared aims or values when there is marital strife. In many a marriage, there is the anguish of not knowing what is for the best — to stay together or to split up, to marry someone else or to avoid re-marriage like the plague? The floods of people at the doors of marriage guidance agencies and a whole range of therapy groups are a measure of how many people no longer have guidelines for their marriages. What is right — to meet my needs, to stay faithful to my partner, not to offend my parents or my employer? All these possible guidelines may conflict with each other. So what to do?

There is one guideline which is obviously paramount, and has the added advantage of probably being the only guideline that your partner subscribes to as well. *The needs of the children must come first.* Innumerable marital struggles have been resolved on this basis, for better or for worse. At first, this usually meant that the couple stayed together, as it was believed to be inevitably damaging for the children to go through the trauma of losing one of the parents, moving house, having to be cared for on a reduced income, enduring the stigma of having divorced parents, and so on. Nowadays, giving priority to 'the needs of the children' often as not means that the couple split, for this is thought to be less traumatic than for the child to wake in the night and hear parents shouting at each other, or to eat every meal in a hostile atmosphere. It may no longer be felt a stigma to have divorced parents if several playmates are likewise situated; and improved divorce settlements for women mean that the mother who takes the child is better able to look after the child materially. Though the practical outcome, splitting or not splitting, may vary from family to family, the moral guideline is constant: what is in the children's interest? For many partners, the agonizing question is not 'Do we part?', but 'What is best for the children?'

Of course, many decisions, either to part or not to part, are taken for other motives, but the reason often given is in terms of the children's needs. And this, as I said at the beginning, is characteristic of all moral codes: sometimes they motivate people, sometimes they are simply the public moral rhetoric of rationalization. And, also as with all moral codes, sometimes there is a guilty conscience. Sometimes the decision is taken to maintain respectability, or to remain faithful to the marriage bed, or to put one's own needs first, and only then does the partner realize that the children are suffering as a result of the decision. He or she feels guilty that they had not put the children first.

Whether the needs of the children motivate the decision, provide a rationalization for it, or induce a guilty conscience after it, in each instance 'the needs of the children' are acting as a moral code. People who say there is no morality these days to guide family life are wrong; the needs of the children form a moral code, even if not commonly recognized as such. They form a code that has emerged as the old moral guidelines have become less and less convincing both to lovers and to parents.

### Educational Needs

If parents are not agreed as to the aims of their marriage and family life, there is even less agreement within society as to the aims of education. We live in a plural, multi-racial, multi-cultural society. Yet we have to send all our children to the same schools. Unless they can afford private schools, negro and Southern white, WASP and Jew, Italian and Chinese all have to send their children to the same public schools in the United States. Welshman and Englishwoman, Pakistani shopkeeper and Cockney factory worker, West Indian unemployed and white racist, they all have to use the same British educational system (though thankfully, the state does allow and fund some minorities, like the Scots, the Anglicans and the Catholics, to run their own schools). All these different groups have differing hopes as to the kind of people they expect their children to grow into, yet they have to be educated in the same schools. Even if there were not this cultural diversity, there would still be considerable disagreement over the goals of education.

Liberals in particular do not want to admit that one of the inescapable functions of education is to prepare children for the economy, which for most children means dead-end jobs on the assembly line or even the dole queue. Many are reluctant to admit that the role of education is to produce factory fodder. There is much talk of 'education for life' (but nobody is agreed what kind of life will face our children thirty years hence, still less what kind of life is desirable); of 'education for leisure' (but attitudes toward work and leisure, and to the prospect of an automated society are very mixed and contradictory); of 'gearing education, especially higher education, toward the needs of the economy' (but this continually comes into conflict with the commitment of many teachers in higher education to knowledge for its own sake and with the commitment to allowing students choice over what they want to study).

Clearly, people are not going to agree on the purpose of education. Yet, with a unitary education system, consensus has to be achieved over the syllabus, staffing levels, investment, and so on. The way to achieve at least the illusion of consensus is to abandon asking what education is *for* and to focus instead on the children and their educational needs, just as parents and child psychologists who do not know their aim in life or what child rearing is for achieve a working consensus by concentrating on the needs of the child. As we have already seen, the one thing people hardly ever ask about a need is what it is for. Teachers, politicians, parents and educational theorists can agree on a set of educational needs that all children have, in the reasonable hope that nobody will upset the apple cart by asking for *what* these are needed. Even political parties of different persuasions will agree about children's needs, at least some of the time. Needs provide surrogate goals when the purpose of life/education/marriage or whatever is unclear. They provide the illusion of consensus where consensus does not exist.

Welfare states in practice tend to provide standardized services, though there is no reason why they have to. In

Britain, there is one kind of state-run education, one health service, one state-run social services department in each town, and so on. Clients may be able to choose to send their child to one state school rather than another one just down the road, to register with one doctor rather than another. But because different schools, doctors, and hospitals do not publicize their goals, clients do not have a real choice. (Choice *could* be possible. Within medicine, for example, there are very different schools of thought on the treatment of schizophrenia, depression, senility, cancer, and *all* the major causes of hospitalization.) If you have a standard provision for all children (or all patients, or all clients) then it is fitting to talk of that provision meeting their 'needs', for the educational needs of children are presumed common to all normal children. Of course, handicapped children, mentally subnormal children, children who do not speak English, perhaps even very bright children, have special needs, but the needs of children are not presumed to vary with the religion, political allegiance or social class of their parents. But as we have seen, these are precisely the things that have to do with our purpose in life, that *do* affect what a parent deems its child to need.

What alternative is there? A plural society could decide to operate a plural system of schools, in which different schools are run explicitly according to different educational philosophies, according to different conceptions of the sort of individuals and the sort of society their sponsors wish to see in the next generation. Every school would be fully supported by taxes (there need be no private schools and no elitism), but parents—and perhaps children—could choose which school best fitted their own life-commitments. They would have an educational 'voucher' that they could spend at any school. Holland already has such a system. The key would not be the 'needs' of the children (which fits a unitary system), but the wants or choices of the parents. This is not to say that the needs of the children would not be taken into account, but they would not become central for lack of any other clear goal. Parents indeed often do not want to be involved, because they too are confused about the goals of schooling. Many prefer the teachers to get on with the job by themselves, secure in the belief that children have needs that professional teachers know how to deal with. Indeed, lack of enthusiasm from parents was a major cause of the dropping of the voucher proposal in Britain.

It is unfortunate that in Britain the voucher idea has been proposed by, and therefore become identified with, the New Right, with the result that it has been rejected out of hand by both centre and left. They are rightly worried that in class-ridden Britain, the proposed voucher system would be used to perpetuate unhealthy class divisions rather than a healthy mix of religions, ethnic and cultural beliefs.

Anthony Flew[8] distinguishes two ways in which professionals, such as teachers, can see the needs of their clients. There is firstly the client-serving professional. Clients, like customers in a shop, state what they want, what their goals are, and the professional or shopkeeper then advises them as to the best means: 'In that case, what you need is . . .' The clients state the desired end, and the professional advises on the means. This is how solicitors and architects operate. 'Please, I want a divorce', 'Please, I want a house built in such and such a place for such and such a price', and the solicitor or architect then informs the client how a divorce may be obtained or the desired house may be built. Such a view of needs would be appropriate to the kind of plural education system I am advocating. When a parent states, 'I want my child brought up a Catholic' or 'I do not want my Puerto Rican child to lose her Spanish tongue and culture', some schools can say, 'Right, we can do as you want. Leave it to us.' Others will say, 'Sorry, not us. Try St Columbine's down the road.'

However, education in most Western countries is not set up that way. Instead, the school sets itself up as what Flew calls the Platonic Guardian, pontificating on ends as well as means. Or rather, it denies parent and child the right to discuss the ends of education, because the school itself dares not reveal its own confusion as to ends. It is not so much that the school *is* a Platonic Guardian, but that it pretends to be. Although a danger with the voucher system is that it can give parents too much control over their children's lives. Some children rightly find their parents' values and horizons too limited, and benefit from the new dimensions added to their lives by a school their parents did *not* choose.

I have noted that making the child and its needs the centre of family life provides nothing outside of itself for the child to

live for as it grows up. A similar problem occurs in schools
that focus on the child's needs rather than on the values and
knowledge the child has to acquire. Up to Grade 6 or
thereabouts in the United States, or at primary school in
Britain, it is possible to centre education on the child. But at
junior high or secondary school, neither teachers, parents nor
children can ignore the brute fact that the child must be fitted
for society, for a job, for running a home perhaps, and that
pretty soon. Somehow the child must be shifted from an
education that panders to its own needs to one that enables
the child to meet the needs of others, which includes the
decidedly abstract needs of entities like the economy and
industry. Is it any wonder that junior high and secondary
school become the main arena for children expressing the
turmoil of adolescence? Nowhere is the shift from Sacred
Child to adult-who-must-fit-in-somehow-or-other more of a
jolt. Is it any wonder that thirteen-year-olds vandalize their
schools? And if the vandals become younger by the decade,
this surely reflects an increasingly early exit from Childhood?

It is often said that the problem is one of authority. Of
course. For the first ten or eleven years of its life, the child's
world revolved around him. The answer to all his whys, 'Why
should I do this?', has been a paternalistic (more likely
maternalistic) 'Because it's best for you, dear', which is how
to tell a child 'Because you need it'. And then preparation for
the brutal world is forced upon him. He has to do lots of
things that conflict with his own needs. He has to learn that
meeting the needs of others and meeting his own needs do
not always mesh (remember, one of the flaws of much modern
need psychology is that it assumes that society is there purely
to meet the needs of the individual, and that conflict between
individual and society is abnormal). So when the thirteen-
year-old demands 'Why?', there is no satisfactory answer. No
wonder there is a problem of authority. No wonder the kid
smashes up the place in his frustration and anger.

### 'What About the Children?'

I have already observed that some mothers refuse to question
whether their relationship to their children should be that of
meeting their needs. I said that this is hardly surprising
because the view of the Child is designed to make the child

dependent on the mother, which is what modern Western motherhood is all about. See the child any other way, and Mum is out of a job.

But perhaps I can persuade parents to reconsider this view of their children after all, for there is one crucial way in which seeing the Child as a bundle of needs backfires against them and takes the care of the Child out of their hands, and this often against their will. The problem with child rearing as meeting the needs of the Child rather than imparting the values of the parents is that, as noted in earlier chapters, needs — especially those that are believed to be universal — are believed to be objective. Just as this enables the parent to put the child's needs above the child's wants, because they are objective rather than subjective and Mummy knows best, so it enables other experts to pontificate on what are children's needs because experts know better than lay people. Baby-care writers, child psychologists, women's magazine writers and school teachers authoritatively tell parents what their children need. Seeing the Child as a bundle of needs greatly enhances the parents' authority over their children (wrested from the factory foreman, the apprentice's master, or the priest) but only at the price of giving most of it away again to the new experts on childhood. As Christopher Lasch puts it, for a few decades the family became a haven in a heartless world, but now it is beseiged. That cold world of business, bureaucracy and professionalism from which the family was once a refuge has now beseiged the family, and in many cases has retaken the Englishman's castle (and, even more so, the American's) by storm.

Chief among these experts on children's needs are teachers. Unlike other experts, teachers have the children in their care six hours a day, half the days of the year; they quickly come to believe that their clients are not the parents, but the children. (It is less easy for a psychologist or baby-care writer to believe that.) And of all clients, children are in the least authoritative position to declare what they want or desire and to resist the findings of experts. Clearly they do resist, but there is no authority behind their resistance, so talk of children's needs can flourish. It affirms the status not only of the teacher over the child, but also over the parent. It provides the illusion to the outside world that there is consensus among teachers; it is in fact the bedrock of the professional unity and authority claimed by teachers.[9]

Parents are increasingly concerned that they seem to have no power to influence their children's schooling. Parent — teacher associations do not give parents any real power, and often are reduced to concerning themselves with fund-raising or serving as a public relations channel by which the school can inform the parents what it is doing. Parents are prone to see this as a problem of a few unresponsive teachers, an education authority that is too remote, or a headteacher who is out of touch or autocratic. What they usually do not understand is that the problem is inherent in a schooling system that puts children's needs first. By elevating their children's needs in their parenting, parents have undermined their own authority. Parents, if you want to influence your school's headteacher, then you must begin by denying that your child's needs are the prime consideration.

Sadly, parents often try to challenge the school by doing exactly the opposite. They claim to know their child's needs better than anyone else ('After all, I am her mother!'), not understanding how little ice this cuts with the teacher ('After all, I am a professional. I haven't worked twenty years in this job for nothing!'). In a voucher system the parent could simply show that the school was not fulfilling what the parent wanted, and remove the child to a school that would, in much the same way as you stop buying from one store and start at another in order to get the goods you want. What would be paramount would be the parents' wishes and values, not the child's needs; *that* is what would give parents leverage over their schools.

Another example of how viewing the children's needs as paramount actually takes power away from the parents is found in the juvenile justice system established in Scotland in 1970. Most children in trouble with the police no longer come before a sheriff, but before a children's panel of three lay men and women whose main concern is to determine not their just deserts for their wrong-doing, but their needs. The stated intention is to have a round-the-table discussion, involving parents and child as well as social workers and other interested parties. The intention is to give the parents more say than under the old system, but the very constitution of the hearing limits this, for anyone (especially the welfare professional) is as competent as the parents to determine the child's needs. Admittedly, the parents can have *some* say, which they could not under the old system. But, at the crunch, parents who have challenged the others present in a children's hearing have discovered that their vote as to the child's needs carries no more weight, and perhaps less, than that of an expert or of a sensible, sensitive lay person.

In this chapter, I have tried to show:
1. how central to child rearing and to education have become the needs of the child;
2. how few query this;
3. how it was introduced historically to increase the status of children and parents;
4. how it functions today as a moral guideline in the absence of others;
5. how it has now come to create problems for both children and parents. The only people who gain unequivocally are teachers and other experts.

In the next chapter, I want to extend our discussion of professionals and clients, of provision and need, of power and dependence, in an examination of need in modern systems of welfare.

# 8: Welfare Needs

The chapters on material needs, needs in work, leisure, marriage and sex have largely concerned the needs of the self and how individuals go about meeting them. The chapter on children described how one of the self's needs, to be a mother, can be intertwined with meeting the needs of children; and the chapter on marriage described how some of a wife's needs are met as she serves her husband's needs.

I am no supporter of those who say that meeting one's own needs is selfish and should be discouraged in favour of meeting the needs of others, which they suppose to be more altruistic, loving, or Christian. I have already shown how teachers are in the business of meeting the educational needs of children, yet this is at the very core of their self-aggrandizement, power over parents, and self-interested disregard for what education is really all about. It is also at the core of some very good teaching .

Meeting your own needs is not necessarily wrong and meeting others' needs is not necessarily good; nor is it always good, as some influenced by an extreme self-ist psychology might say, to meet your own needs, and wrong to meet others'. Things just are not that simple. I want to be as critical of meeting others' as one's own needs; there is more that links than separates the two. Both imply a human race with no meaning or purpose outside of itself; both involve a morality that is powerful and seductive to people in the modern West, but which causes all kinds of problems for us.

Meeting the needs of their clients is central to the way in which the helping professions (teachers, doctors, nurses, social workers, etc.) see their work. Meeting need is one of their chief aims, at least according to their official philosophy. So it seems likely that we can learn a lot about the nature of need by looking at the practice of welfare.

Although welfare agencies are formally set up to meet people's needs (whether medical, social or educational), need is by no means what always motivates clients to approach an agency. More typically they come with a problem, not a need.

*Patient:* 'I can't see very well out of my right eye.'
*Optician:* 'What you need is glasses. I'll prescribe you some.'

*Client:* 'I can't cope with my mother at home any more. She's senile and incontinent.'
*Social worker:* 'You need a district nurse and a home help, and some appliances around the house. If they are not enough, she'll need hospitalization.'

*Parent:* 'Johnny's not getting on very well at school, is he?'
*Teacher:* 'I think he needs some remedial teaching. I'll arrange it.'

It is part of the practice of social work to convert the client's presenting problem into an underlying need. Only then can action be taken. The doctor does not expect patients to diagnose their own medical needs; that is the doctor's job. Patients are supposed only to know that they are in pain or unable to cope; sometimes, as in mass screening for cancer, the patient may not be aware that anything is wrong at all. Teachers do not expect parents to know what their children's educational needs are. Clients approach the agency with goals that they cannot achieve by themselves (seeing properly, coping with mother), and the professional advises as to what is needed to achieve that goal.

That is the theory, at any rate. The professional is the one qualified to assess and then meet the need. But is this actually how needs are assessed and met? My examples will be mainly from social work, but I am not aware of any evidence that similar processes do not operate in other professions such as medicine and teaching.

### Assessing Need
In a busy agency that deals with hundreds or thousands of clients a year, there must be routines to help with the assessment of need. Not every Tom, Dick or Harry can walk off the street directly into the office of a social worker or a doctor's surgery. The receptionist, who first takes his name and address and makes some preliminary enquiries, may discover straight away that he's come to the wrong place;

perhaps he should have come not to the social work department but to the social security office because that is where unemployment benefit, or old age pensions, or whatever it is he is asking about is dealt with. Many clients have not been to the agency before, or not for a long time; they may misunderstand the purpose of the agency, or not realize how serious their problem has to be before the agency will take them seriously. (I have not been to a doctor for fifteen years, and haven't a clue now how ill I have to be before I can go to a doctor without being rapped over the knuckles for wasting his time.)

So, for clients who present themselves to an agency (rather than being referred by another agency), the first assessor of their need, indeed of whether they have what the agency would count as a need at all, is not a professional worker but the receptionist.

The receptionist may then arrange for the client to see a social worker or doctor. As the receptionist is not competent to diagnose his need in detail, she cannot know which social worker or docto in the agency is best suited to meet the client's need. It is a tenet of social work that not all social workers can help all clients, and part of assessment is getting the client allocated to the most appropriate social worker. In Britain, where there are generic social work departments that deal with a wide range of social need, it is recognized that some social workers are better with rowdy youngsters, others with doddery old men just out of hospital, still others with young pregnant girls, and so on.

In one generic Scottish social work agency studied most carefully by Gilbert Smith,[1] an agency with an excellent reputation, the receptionist would pass the client on to a duty social worker who interviewed him and prepared an initial report. This was then presented to an allocation meeting the next morning, in which it was decided that the client (in absentia) either became a case and was allocated to a worker, or that no further action was necessary. This procedure was designed to get the client to the best worker as quickly as possible.

What guidelines were used in determining the clients' need? If the client or a member of his family had been to the agency before, even several years before, he would be in the file already; there would already be some definition of need, and a note of who had dealt with him then. This often influenced who he was allocated to the next time, as continuity was felt to be a good thing: but this would often be decided before, indeed in place of, any assessment of his current need. Or, because a female client had changed her name since she was last at the agency, the receptionist might not notice that she had been a client before; she might therefore get allocated to someone other than her previous social worker. Since the agency had three teams covering different areas of the town, the client's address was important in determining who he was allocated to; a change of address *and* a change of name almost certainly would lead to an old client being dealt with by a new social worker.

These things could all be interpreted as mistakes. But they were not mistakes, they were inevitable, because the agency faced a dilemma: on the one hand it had a commitment to matching the special needs of each client to the particular skills of a social worker; on the other hand, as most clients came to the agency in some distress, it was important to classify and allocate them as speedily as possible. If they were mistakes, then they were hardly ever queried at a later date. Smith concluded that they were not mistakes, but that, throughout the agency, need was not an attribute of clients at all, but a product of the pressures and routines of the agency.

He found further evidence for this in the allocation meeting itself. There was virtually no discussion there of the particular skills of individual workers and whether they were suitable for the clients under discussion, even though this was supposed to be the purpose of the meeting. In fact, the meeting was not about that at all. Rather the aim of each social worker was to come out of the meeting (a) without having increased his or her caseload too much, at the same time as (b) not having seemed to shirk, and (c) having maintained at least a smattering of all kinds of cases in his caseload, because the agency was committed to each worker having a generic caseload.

That need had become a product of agency boundaries had been understood by the architects of these new generic departments when they were set up. Ten years earlier, there had been separate children's departments, probation departments, home help organizations, and so on; a person with multiple problems would end up in one agency and get labelled as having one particular need with the result that his other needs were left unmet, or he would become the client of several agencies and several workers would end up dealing with a single family. Thus the actual service clients got was determined by the structure of the agencies and their interrelations, rather than by client need.

The new unified departments were meant to change all that. At last, the service a client received could be determined by his need alone. Smith considers that this intention completely misunderstands the nature of need. Not only was need never a characteristic of the client; it never could be. Once a particular social service had got off the ground, need could never be anything other than a product of organizational routines and structures. An agency may be initiated in response to a need; but once set up, it will only define as a need some problem the client has that the agency can do something about. It is the mandate of the agency that determines whether the client has the need.

This is quite in line with the imputation of needs in other areas. 'You're a sinner who needs Jesus' is, to anyone other than a believer, a product of a particular kind of theology rather than a characteristic of individuals. And even to an evangelist, you only need Jesus because of what he has done for you on the cross: your need for him could hardly be said to exist unless he had done something about it. Or you have a pain, and the physician decides you need to be put on a kidney machine; you certainly did not need a kidney machine before kidney machines were invented. Your need for a machine is a product of modern medicine as much as of your pain, and could not be otherwise.

## Meeting Need
Many social workers, doctors and other caring professionals are genuinely motivated by their desire to meet human need. But when it comes to deciding how to treat a particular client or patient, they are all too aware that simply diagnosing the client's needs will not necessarily tell them what to do. There are at least three reasons why this is so.[2]

The client may have several needs, conflicting with each other; or the client's needs may conflict with those of other family members or of neighbours; or with those of the social worker. (Remember, the social worker is committed to meeting not only the client's needs but also those of his or her own family.) So when a homeless person comes to a social worker late on a Friday afternoon wanting housing, and the worker has committed herself to taking her own children out that evening, what does she do? Either the needs of her children or those of the client must go by the board. The self-sacrificing wives of some doctors and clergy know this experience all too well, as do their children.

This raises an interesting possibility. Perhaps need can only act as a guideline in moral and practical decision-making when there are relatively few needs or one paramount need, as with the needs of the children in many marital trials. But because welfare professionals are surrounded by need on all sides, need can no longer be relied upon to provide guidance. Needs are expanding in all areas, but welfare has to face now the sort of problems that other institutions (like marriage or work) may not have to face for a decade or two more. Perhaps this is why welfare, more than any other field, has generated sensible philosophical discussion of 'need' and whether there is some better way of conceiving of people's many problems and requirements.[3]

Secondly, even if it is clear what the client's need is, it may not be clear who should provide for it. Should it be the social worker or some other agency? Perhaps it should be the client himself? Indeed, social workers often feel that the client has brought his woes upon himself and should sort them out himself: the old distinction between the deserving and the undeserving poor is far from dead. Then perhaps the client's family should take responsibility? In Elizabethan England, and today in Yugoslavia and in Israel, the law requires that children look after their own parents; Mrs Thatcher currently wants Britain to move more in this direction. Just because an old person is shown to be in need does not in itself demand that the social services do something; it all depends on the country and its particular values and particular kind of family life.

An example of the third problem is provided by the Department of Health and Social Security (DHSS), the agency in Britain responsible for handing out supplementary benefit, the cash benefit available to the poorest of those on welfare. I have observed earlier that a need must always be *for* something. Needs are triadic: a person X needs Z for purpose Y. Ian Sinclair has pointed out that:[4]

The problem in social services is that the nature of Y is usually obscure; in so far as it is not, a great many Zs could lead to it, and none of these will do so with any certainty . . .

This type of uncertainty can lead to the concept of need losing, or at least altering, its triadic status. Take, for example, the Exceptional Needs Payments which are made from time to time by the DHSS to clients on Supplementary Benefit. If, for example, a client is moving house, he or she is wise to draw up a list of items required to furnish the new house (e.g. curtains), cost them and negotiate with the DHSS over the money necessary to pay for them. The needs in this case are presumably curtains, etc, but it is usually obscure what they are needed for (is it warmth, privacy, or self-respect?). For this reason, argument about the likely effects of this or that amount of money are not very persuasive with the DHSS. Their officers usually have a picture of the sort of expenditure allowed in these circumstances, and adhere to a tariff. Needs are treated as entitlements or deserts.

Whereas entitlements and deserts are also triadic concepts, the logical relationships of the triad seem to be different from those which occur in the case of 'needs'. One can compare 'X needs Z in order to obtain Y' with 'X is entitled to Z because X is in situation Y'. My guess is that in dealing with individual cases and perhaps also in forming policy, the DHSS has largely shifted from a concept of 'need' to one of 'entitlement', while often retaining the language of 'need'. If this is so, one reason for it could be the fact that the relationship between Z and Y implied by 'need' is too uncertain to satisfy the DHSS's requirements for clear rules and fair procedures.

We have already seen how ignoring the end (Y) converts the means (the need, Z) into an end in its own right. Many, many needs are of this nature; strictly speaking they are entitlements or rights. Indeed, this is how many people conceive of human needs. It is not at all clear what a husband needs sex *for*, so in the absence of some end beyond the act itself, sex becomes an entitlement. What children need education for (certainly beyond the three Rs) is not at all clear, so their need for education takes on the character of an entitlement. Likewise the child's need for love; most mothers would not be able to articulate what their child needs love *for*, but that he needs it they have not the slightest doubt. Indeed, needs are so frequently of this kind that it would go against common usage to cease calling them needs; needs are powerful precisely *because* they lose their formal, logical triadic structure (something that will be explored in chapter 10).

It should be clear from all this that the official rhetoric that welfare identifies and meets needs does not and cannot fit what actually happens. Rarely does the professional worker advise clients concerning what they need to resolve a stated problem; rather the worker advises as to what standard procedures, treatments, technologies or payments are available. I suspect this is as true of the highly trained doctor as of the rather less sophisticated clerk in the DHSS.

## How Needs Change

I have said that many welfare professionals are genuinely caring people who identify an unmet need that they pasionately believe should be met. But I have also noted in the chapters on sex and parenthood how needs are identified or invented for political purposes. The two statements are not necessarily contradictory. It is not incompatible to say that a mother genuinely is concerned to meet the needs of her child, *and* that the notion of the child as a bundle of needs has been used politically in order to protect children and to enhance the status of motherhood.

Even the most simplistic political analysis reveals that people's understandings of what counts as a person in need vary for political reasons. The fundamental reason is as follows. Although it is usually true that the client needs the professional (the patient needs the doctor to get well, the client needs the solicitor to get a divorce), in the last analysis something else is even more true: the professional needs the client.

Most human beings in history have done without doctors and lawyers, but no doctors or lawyers have ever got by without patients and clients. Those who feel ill could go to a religious official (witch doctor, priest) in order to find out how they had offended God or neighbour and repent; or they could go to a grandmother for some time-honoured remedy; or to some unqualified 'quack'; or to a modern, scientifically trained doctor; or they could simply hope for the best. For many diseases (notably those that take up most of the modern doctor's time: depression, mental illness, rheumatism and arthritis, and many little niggles of old age), there is not much evidence that any one course of action is that much more effective than any other. If people believe they need a doctor for such ailments, this is surely not unrelated to the ever increasing prestige of medicine over the last hundred and fifty years. I personally think that modern medicine is, on the whole, very much a good thing, but that people feel they *need* modern medicine is as much a feature of the status of the modern medical profession as of their ailing bodies.

This is even more obviously true of lawyers. You don't *need* a lawyer to get a divorce or buy a house; you could do it yourself, or get a friend to act on your behalf; but lawyers make us believe we need them. Where else would they get their bread and butter?

This ultimate need of the professions has three consequences. First, they attempt to exclude non-members from practising; if they cannot succeed in reducing, or hopefully completely eliminating, competition, then they may be out of a job.

Secondly, because professionals ultimately need their clients more than their clients need them, they put up a smokescreen, a rhetoric, that talks only of the client's need for them. This is comparable to the process discussed in the chapter on marriage where, if the woman is economically dependent on the man, it is in her interest to become the expert in personal and emotional matters and to induce all kinds of emotional needs in her man. (This is not to say that she does not love her man, any more than it is to say that the doctor is not dedicated to his patients.)

There are some exceptions to this. If a profession has insufficient resources and is becoming swamped with demands by clients, it will not go out of its way to convince people they are in need, and will often refer clients on to other agencies. Social work seems to be in this position at the moment in Britain.

Third, though professionals do not want to be swamped with demands, they do want a steadily increasing level of need. My local county council has just announced proudly that its 'meals on wheels' scheme, delivering hot meals to elderly and infirm people at home, is expanding: 'When begun in 1974, just over 850,000 meals were delivered. By the end of 1984, the service could be delivering up to one million meals a year.' It is seen as an achievement that more people now should have recognized their inability to cook for themselves. Something would be wrong if the service were not expanding. As William Blake put it a hundred and fifty years ago,

> Pity would be no more
> If we did not make somebody poor,
> And mercy no more could be
> If all were as happy as we.[5]

It is crucial for there to be a waiting list for any professional service, otherwise the need for that service may come into question. But it is crucial also that the waiting list is not too long, otherwise the competence of the profession will come into question (as is at present the case with the British National Health Service — right-wingers lay the blame for lengthy waiting lists on the militant unionism of auxiliary health workers and on the nationalized system of health care itself, and some are beginning to argue for the dismantling of the NHS).

One way of maintaining the waiting list at a respectable length is for the profession or authority quietly to keep on changing the definition of what entitles you to get onto the list. In other words, the definition of need. In one city I know well, the city's Housing Department that provides housing for lower-income families distinguishes the demand for housing from the need for housing. Because the Department is part of the city's welfare services, it is in the business of meeting need, not each and every demand. So, single people whose parents live less than forty miles from the city are not deemed to need housing (it is assumed they can live with their parents and commute), though separated child-less people with similarly close parents *are* deemed to need housing. Such arbitary definitions can be easily manipulated to maintain a respectable waiting list and avoid public uproar at a council that could at any time be deemed to be building either too many or too few houses.

Quiet manipulation of the figures maintains control in the hands of the bureaucrats. An alternative would be to put all the expressed desires for a house onto the waiting list, and then it would be possible for all to see what are the housing requirements of the population, and priorities can then be determined democratically. Typically this is not done. Professions and bureaucrats cannot control demand in the way they can control need. Because need is something that can be determined by expertise, surveys, etc., they can maintain a monopoly on the right to define need.

This is well understood by those who feel they are in need but are not deemed so by the authority. The single woman in her thirties who does not get on particularly well with her parents, who in any case live twenty miles and three bus rides from her work, may well feel she needs accommodation. Privately rented accommodation is virtually unavailable, and she cannot afford to buy. But she finds she is constantly banging her head against the brick wall of the Housing Department, who simply say that, according to their rules, she is not in need. It may not actually get her accommodation, but it would be considerably more pleasant to be informed that her request has been added to the list but unfortunately the council does not have sufficient resources to be likely to meet the demand.

The amount of money available to an agency is often out of their control. The government of the day may be cutting back on public services or expanding them, and local hospitals, social services, housing departments, and the like have to scale their provision up or down accordingly. It should be clear by now that 'need', much more than rights or demands, enables them to do this with the minimum of public fuss. As with the needs of children, needs have historically been crucial for enhancing the position of the poor, the sick and the under-privileged. But as with children, there is mounting evidence that seeing them as in need may no longer always serve their best interests.

### Alternatives

How else may the poor, the sick and the under-privileged be seen that *does* serve their best interests?

One way is to place a new emphasis on the wishes, desires and demands of the client. As discussed in the last chapter concerning schooling, this would necessitate a choice of agencies to which the client could go; a measure of competition would enable clients to use their feet to express dissatisfaction with a service. And it would give professional workers greater scope to articulate and put into practice their own most deeply held beliefs. Being a Christian social worker or doctor, for example, would not be simply a matter of the person's *attitude* to the job; Christian workers could actually create alternative forms of service, and if their beliefs have any truth in them then they should find a demand for their services. Likewise other radicals; instead of fruitlessly fighting the system from within, they could experiment with a real alternative.

Clients could then say to the agency, 'I want your help in educating my child / getting safely through my pregnancy / building my house, but I want you to use and take notice of my own values and skills.' They want an agency whose motto is 'We're here to help you' rather than 'You need us'.

A good example of what usually happens, though, is provided by the police in Britain. Policing was in medieval times the responsibility of all citizens; sometimes they would take turns in keeping watch, somewhat like military service. By the eighteenth century it became apparent that full-time watchmen would have to be appointed, but the legal framework was, and substantially still is, that the full-time police force is there to help the citizen to keep the peace. But this is not how the police see themselves today. Posters and PR pamphlets constantly talk of how *the public* can help *the police.* And the public and politicians concur in this; there are frequent calls for the police to 'do something' about the latest crime wave, whether it be muggings, political killings, or whatever. The medieval notion that it is ordinary people who keep the peace has been completely — and in my opinion disastrously[6] — lost in practice. Citizens' competence in looking after themselves is being abdicated in favour of a need for professional policing.

Another alternative is to make explicit that many needs have in practice become rights or entitlements. This has two advantages. One is that it restores to clients some measure of influence with the professional. It is up to the clients whether or not they take up their entitlement, whereas with needs this is not always so, as some psychiatric patients are all too painfully aware.

The other advantage is that rights and entitlements are known to inhere in the individual only as a result of his or her being a member of the human race or as a result of legislation enacted to protect citizens in a particular country. It relates the individual to a community. Needs, on the other hand, pretend to exist within the individual without reference to anyone else, while in fact the identification of needs rests very largely with agencies that are not answerable to the individual.

It would not be desirable to eliminate the notion of need altogether from welfare services. The under-privileged often do not know their rights, or even sometimes their wants, and agencies dedicated to their needs do afford them some protection. Consumerist models of welfare (based on demand or rights), assume informed, intelligent citizens, and not all citizens are or can be. Probably some combination of rights, claims, interests, obligations, desires *and* needs is required in the moral vocabulary of welfare.[7] What seems to be desirable is that welfare geared to meeting needs should provide a safety net for those who, even in an informed and free society, are not able to articulate or get their rights.

The tendency, however, in a society that glorifies need and that employs the language of need to cover all social relations is the opposite: to let paternalistic welfare enter more and more spheres of life, for it seems the natural candidate. More and more problems, personal and social, are believed to be resolved by some kind of therapy, and the medical/psychiatric view of the human being eases out other views (for example, the view that we are morally responsible). Once therapy has replaced morality in the spirit of the age, the door is wide open for welfare services to take over every area of our lives; or perhaps as welfare services expand, so this encourages this therapeutic spirit. Where *everything* is conceived of as a need, then every area of our lives may be scrutinized by the experts in defining need. An ideology that claims to put the individual first ends up submitting him entirely to the experts and the bureaucrats, and Orwell's 1984 is upon us.

The other danger is that to analyse critically the idea of needs as I have done leads some to think that therefore welfare services should be dismantled! Many people in Britain at the time of writing are aware of the lack of accountability of teachers, doctors and social workers, and this may have something to do with the widespread support for Mrs Thatcher's programme to 'get the welfare state off people's backs'.

However, I must stress that I cannot support such a programme of dismantling the welfare state. There is considerable evidence that the National Health Service has acted as a valuable brake on the power of doctors; and the bureaucratic control of education, social work and other welfare services has surely had a similar restraining effect on professional autonomy. In the United States, where doctors and hospitals are in the business of making a profit, there is far more pressure to expand medical needs, and hence profits, than in Britain. Nowhere is this more visible than in California where the rash of private psychotherapy is a direct cause of the expansion of the psychological needs of those Californians with money to spare.

Mrs Thatcher's policies have two main motives: to reduce government expenditure, and to apply the principles of the marketplace to human welfare. Both these motives raise economic doctrines above people—in particular, the poorest and weakest people in Britain—and this is very different from what I am saying in this chapter. If I am looking carefully at some aspects of the welfare state, it is because it may not guarantee the rights or serve the best interests of some of its clients. The last thing they need is to be treated as playthings of an unproven economic ideology.

In this chapter, I have not been so concerned with documenting whether people do or do not have needs; we already have libraries of books documenting people's needs. I have been concerned here with need as it is used in practice, for this is what need *is*. My aim has been to show the functions of conceiving people as in need; how need functions ideologically and politically; how people hope and claim that need will provide practical and moral guidelines for action, yet need is decreasingly able to do so. If one of the burdens of. previous chapters is that need provides a new morality which people hope will tell them how to behave, the lesson of welfare is that need will not serve too well in such a role; its imperatives are rarely all that clear.

# Intermezzo

In Part One I have documented how widespread the language of need has become, not only in the everyday language of ordinary people, but also in the language of experts, politicians, professionals and academics. This much is surely indisputable. It is a fact.

What *is* disputable are two things. One is whether this language of need actually corresponds to real needs, or whether it is just a form of expression? When someone says 'I need self-realization/a doctor/work/a new car', is this just a way of saying 'I want such and such', or do people actually need doctors and work and cars to an extent they did not before? The answer to this varies somewhat from need to need, but in general I think the new language of need does correspond to new structures of need. Capitalism and the professions (including such professions as motherhood) can only survive by actually putting people in need. This is not so much a fact, as a conclusion that is drawn in the light of the facts, and throughout Part One I have been drawing such a conclusion.

The other disputable conclusion is a related one: that the language of need corresponds to people actually experiencing themselves in need. When people say they need something, generally they mean it. Sometimes, they are aware that they will hardly die if some of their fancier needs are not met, but these are the more trivial instances. People are not joking usually when they say they need to self-actualize themselves or that their child needs love and security; when a man says he needs work, or a woman says people need to be needed.

If my readers are convinced only by my documentation of the language of need, and have reservations about the conclusion that the language corresponds to structures and experiences of need, I hope they will not give up reading. The language of need is as important as the structure and experience of need, if not more so, and is central to the rest of the book. Indeed, if the language of need does *not* reflect structural need and personal experiences of need, then it becomes doubly curious why this language should flourish? Why should people talk of themselves and others as in need if in reality they are not, or do not experience themselves as such?

So, we have documented the breadth of need and its apparently inexorable expansion. Why has this come about? What is the power and the plausibility of seeing ourselves in need? Why do people talk of being in need? Why do they welcome being in need? What does need mean to people? Is it indeed desirable to be in need? Is there a common denominator that links the incredibly varied sorts of needs that have been documented? In a nutshell, what is need really all about? Clearly, one has to go beyond simple documentation of the facts to answer such questions, and that is what the rest of the book is about.

I have often referred in Part One to the ideological functions of need, how it serves the interests of professions and business, and how it serves to maintain social institutions such as work and marriage. It has been relatively easy for me to talk in these terms, because this is how critics today generally analyse needs. But, as I hope to show in the next chapter, this does not provide anything like a totally adequate explanation for the popularity and plausibility of need.

We must also look at the *meaning* of need for ordinary people. It is not just that greedy institutions like businesses and the family get people to consume and conceive by putting them in need and then convincing them that consumption or conception are the way to meeting such needs. That would be at best only half the truth; at worst, a nice trendy sociological fairy tale. No, people *get themselves* to consume and conceive; they really love having their needs; they would not want it any other way. Without their needs, they would not be able to make sense of their lives; without their needs, their lives would have no structure, or so they believe.

It is historically demonstrable that needs are often created for economic or political purposes. This has been said and done before. What I believe has not been fully understood is the way in which, once created, needs play an important moral function. They provide a way of talking about morals, a set of criteria for justifying our actions. *This*, I believe, is what all modern needs have in common, and this is what I want to explore further in the following chapters. Exactly *how* does need provide a morality? How does it provide, or give the impression of providing, imperatives?

# PART TWO
# NEED: REALITY OR MORALITY?

# 9: Explaining Need

That needs and talk of needs have proliferated in the twentieth century has been observed by many. Nobody with their eyes open could fail to notice it. But how to account for it? What is this phenomenon all about?

## Needs as Progress

The most common account of needs is that they reflect progress. As civilization advances, so needs expand; indeed, it is their expansion that makes life richer and fuller. If new needs did not emerge as old ones are met, then we would stagnate: the economy would stagnate, individual personalities would stagnate, society would stagnate. A need is inherently good and is its own justification; if something is a need, it is obviously good. This is so commonly assumed that I need hardly give examples.

But there are problems with this account of the expansion of needs. Firstly, it is hard to believe that all the needs documented in Part One are advances. Apparently we need nuclear weapons for our defence; even if necessary (and that is debatable) it is surely not good, nor an advance. That five thousand elderly people in my home county need meals on wheels, is that a good thing? That men need sex — how much comfort is that to the rape victim?

If only one need could be shown not to be a good thing (and many more can be), then this makes nonsense of the assumption that it is the necessity of needs that makes them good things and the result of progress. In Hitler's eyes, the final solution was necessary to solve the Jewish problem. No, what makes some needs good things — and some undoubtedly are — is not the fact that they are needs, but that we approve of the goal for which they are needed and that there are no other more preferred means to that goal. Necessity cannot replace ethics, at least not logically. However, it is not logic that gives needs their power and plausibility, as we shall see in the next chapter.

Secondly, whatever else they are, many 'needs' are clearly not needs; that is, they are not necessary, or it is not at all clear what they are necessary for. This is obvious with some 'needs', as 99 per cent of viewers of some of the more ludicrous TV commercials know perfectly well. But it is also true of many so-called basic human needs. Employment and education are often cited in United Nations circles as basic human needs, but just why self-sufficient peasant communities need city-based teachers trained in Western methods (and show me a teacher who wasn't), or why they need to become dependent on a world market over which they have no control (which is what employment and entry into a money economy mean), is not at all clear. Or take Erich Fromm's five existential needs: relatedness, transcendence, rootedness/security, identity, and a frame of orientation. Philosopher Patricia Springborg notes:

> If we look carefully at the catalogue of existential needs that he gives, we find that there is little or no point in calling them needs at all. What he is presenting is a set of cultural values or normative stipulations. If the requirements of relatedness, transcendence, rootedness, identity and a frame of orientation and devotion were really 'needs', man would show a greater propensity to satisfy them, if not indeed a compulsion.[1]

Thirdly, many needs are deemed good because they are natural. But few needs are demonstrably dictated by biology. Many of course, such as sex, have a biological connection; but any man who claims that biology drove him to rape a woman, or any judge who accepts such a plea, has abandoned man's undoubted capacity for responsibility and self-control and sees him as no different from other animals. Many men have been celibate for life, and there is no evidence that their lives have been impoverished in comparison to the sexually active; only those who believe from the start that men need to have an active sex life can interpret the evidence so as to support this belief.

We do have a need for food and drink. Our bodies clearly dictate this. But that explains virtually nothing about our eating habits. It doesn't explain why I eat what I eat, or when I eat. I ate roast beef and Yorkshire pudding last Sunday lunchtime, but that has virtually nothing to do with any biological need, and has virtually everything to do with the culture of white Englishmen living in the mid-twentieth century. So our need to eat does not force us into any particular act of eating. If you want final proof, look at

Gandhi, Bobby Sands or any other hunger striker.

This is not to minimize biology, but simply to say that the relation between biology and human behaviour is rarely that of necessity. Even when it is, as in urinating when the bladder is full, the meaning given to the act (for example, whether it is shameful) and the rules surrounding it vary widely from culture to culture. Any Englishman can see that merely by crossing the Channel to France, Americans simply by crossing the Rio Grande.

If not all needs are necessary or good, you may reply that some good things clearly are needs. But, and this is the fourth problem, how would you know? Clearly, I need fuel if my car is to run, because I have seen the consequences of it running out of fuel. But what about Fromm's need for relatedness? Have you ever known someone who didn't relate to others? If some such person did exist, how would you ever meet him? Or, how little would you have to relate to others before you would count as not relating? The whole issue is full of absurdities, vaguenesses and questions that can only be answered by introducing values.

After these four objections, there really is not much that remains of the notion that needs are by definition good and a mark of progress. Undoubtedly, many needs are the product of Western civilisation, but whether that means they are a mark of progress is a value judgement. For my money, some needs *are* a mark of progress, but this is very far from saying that the mass expansion of needs in recent decades may be explained, and therefore justified, as a mark of progress.

**Needs as Ideology**
Whereas the view of needs as progress considers that new needs are continually *discovered,* an alternative view sees them as continually *created* in order to keep institutional structures going. Capitalism needs new markets if it is to expand, so it generates new needs. Producers need consumers, so they try to make sure the consumers need them. Capital needs labour, so it persuades labour that it needs work. Professionals need clients, so they create a monopoly in which clients need them. Mothers need children, so they persuade themselves that their children need them.

The basic theory here is simple. If person X needs person Y, then it is a neat solution for X to work on Y so that Y ends up needing X. Or, even if you can't get Y actually to need you, then work on his mind so that he believes that he needs you. This theory is basic to Marxist and socialist understandings of society: ultimately the powerful need the powerless more than the powerless need them. Why then do the powerless not rise up in revolt? Because through ideology (the structure of ideas and experience created by the powerful), the powerless believe that they actually need the powerful, they believe that they need the system as it is.

This understanding of need as ideology has taken various forms, and is perhaps best known in the writings of Wilhelm Reich, Herbert Marcuse, and Ivan Illich. Clearly, I myself have used an ideological understanding of needs in Part One, to some extent at least. However, though I consider that needs are constructed by human beings for specific purposes, there do seem to be serious limitations to the thesis that they are created by the powerful to control the powerless. There may be some truth in that thesis, but it cannot possibly be the whole story. Why?

Firstly, capitalism appears to produce many needs that it cannot satisfy; governments fall because they cannot fulfil the promises they make; education does not neatly slot people into the jobs the economy requires. There is dissatisfaction precisely because people's needs are not met.[2] Some Marxists would reply to this that this is precisely the intention of capitalism, to meet each need only partly, forever promising that just one more commodity will fill the need fully.[3] But I think the criticism of the Marxist position holds; capitalism does *not* appear to be in control of itself.

Secondly, all Marxist critics of need set up new needs. Dismissing the needs of the capitalists, they replace them with, for example, the needs of growth psychology. Instead of the needs of capital, attention is directed to what is really needed if the human personality is to flourish. The arbitary and artificial needs produced by capitalism must be replaced by what human beings genuinely need if they are to become truly *human* beings. The New Left believes in these needs even more passionately than everyone else believes they need cars, dead-end jobs and wives. But every need brought out of the New Left hat is as suspect as the old needs; the New Left too has joined the Enlightenment bandwagon that believes the discovery of ever higher needs to be progress. It simply disagrees as to which *are* the higher needs. So, therefore, the new needs are as problematic as the old ones:

(a) It is not at all clear that all these new needs are progress. Fromm's need for transcendence, for example, can be met by either art or destruction, his need for rootedness by either matriarchy or patriarchy, fraternity or incest.[4] There is nothing inherently progressive about these needs. It all depends how they are met.

(b) Whatever else they are, clearly not all these needs are needs. Humans have got along without them for millennia. And if the answer be that they *are* necessary for a fully human existence, well then we are into the question of values — 'What is a fully human existence?' The crunch is not the needs, but the values that make them necessary.

(c) It is not possible to root these needs in biology or some demonstrable human essence; no, they are rooted in values.

Thirdly, these so-called critics of need tend to assume that people are dupes. How else can people believe they need things so manifestly against their own interests? Herbert Marcuse, for example, has often been criticized for élitism in his thinking — only he and a few other radicals can see through the game, and so this select band of intellectuals will have to run the revolution until the masses can be educated to see clearly for themselves. Only then can they be trusted to determine their own needs.

Ivan Illich escapes this criticism. He notes that people are all too aware of the gap between what they want and what capitalism offers them; there is much dissatisfaction, and much of it takes a political form. The false needs of capitalism are not so embedded in the psyche of the masses that they are rendered incapable of moral judgement. All this is surely true, but Illich's alternative seems suspect too. He seems to view people as autonomous, somehow able to know their own needs independently of the society they live in. Well, I agree that people are not idiots, but neither are they Robinson Crusoes

So, the problem persists: how do ordinary people come to believe in their needs? Why should people submit to ideology? Wilhelm Reich pointed the way to an answer by synthesizing Marx's notion of the false consciousness of the masses with Freud's notion of the person's unconscious. The sexual needs of the person are repressed and find expression in other,

artificial needs. Freud thought that this process of sublimation
was what produced civilization; Reich said that it was what
enabled an oppressive society to keep its members in
thraldom. Freud's contribution was to demonstrate what
makes these sublimated needs so powerful: they are
substitutes for sexuality, and therefore cannot be ignored.
This, then, explains the prolonged continuance of a capitalism
whose overthrow Marx had predicted would be relatively
speedy.

This is a nice psychoanalytic tale, but it can be believed
only if you accept its assumptions about the primacy of
sexual needs. (Incidentally, Freud himself did not make this
assumption; he saw the sexual needs of the id and the
conscience of the superego, the id's pleasure principle and the
ego's reality principle, as equal and in perpetual struggle.)
You have to accept hook-line-and-sinker a view of the
biological power behind sexual needs that I have been at
pains in this book to show is itself a classic form of ideology.
So, Reich's theory is fine as a justification for liberating your
sexual urges from the restraints of your conscience, for it tells
you that this is no mere self-indulgence but a politically
progressive act that casts off the weight of oppression. But it
hardly solves the problems in the notion of need.

There is a further problem with Reich's theory and with its
development by Fromm and Marcuse. If it were correct, then
how would people be able to resist ideology, as Illich so
clearly shows they do? How would people be able to see
through ideology, as Marcuse and his many thousands of
disciples so clearly do?

Further, this theory supposes political and psychological
processes manifestly at odds with people's real interests; if
human life were at root flawed, this would be plausible. But
Marcuse and company have a blithely optimistic view of
human beings, and especially of their reason. So it is just not
plausible that people should behave, and be psychologically
constituted, in a way so manifestly detrimental to themselves.
No, people's subjection to need, to ideology, must be because
there is something in it for them.

## Needs as Morality
In my view of needs as a system of morals, I believe it is
possible to show what is in it for people, to see how and why

ordinary, sensible, rational people can subject themselves to need.

There is one feature of some of the major writings on need that points towards need as a form of morality. Marx, Fromm, Maslow and others have noted the incompatibility between human beings orienting their lives to meeting their needs, and a traditional Christianity that would deny the needs of the self and would give charity to others not because their needs entitled them to it but out of sheer disinterested love. The non-religious humanism of these writers would replace religion with service and self-fulfilment making life the project of responding to human need. They are clear about this.

I suspect that they are correct in seeing Christianity and the exaltation of need as opposed. But it is not that easy to do without the kind of moral framework that Christianity has provided. They are perhaps too close to the needs they espouse to see that their system of humanistic needs provides just such a substitute morality,[5] and that it is perhaps *this* feature of need that gives it its appeal. Life as a project of meeting needs becomes almost a substitute, disguised religion. Religion and morality are no longer fashionable, so new religions and new moralities have to be introduced under another name.

Before exploring this further in chapter 10, one further requirement for an adequate theory of needs must be noted. Almost all criticisms of need end up in either a Left or a Right political position. There is the Left position that criticizes the big corporations for manipulating our wants, while ignoring the manipulation of the masses by the Leftist élite that would run their proposed Leninist society. And there is the Right position that criticizes the élitism of the Left, the paternalism and uniformity of the welfare state, and argues for the free choice of the consumer, while ignoring how these supposedly free choices are subtly but grossly manipulated by the big corporations and the ideology of modern society. It seems to me that neither view is tenable as the whole story. I have already in Part One drawn on both, but any satisfactory theory of need must not exclude any needs from the microscope, and that is the fatal flaw of both Left and Right: they dismiss needs they disapprove of, and are entirely uncritical of the needs they approve of.

When in chapters 12 and 13 I look at positive alternatives

to need, the temptation will be even greater to slide into the camp of either Left or Right. I will doubtless succumb to this temptation to some extent, for all the alternatives have usually been presented in and moulded by a Left/Right political context; and undoubtedly there is something to be gained from alternatives proposed by both Left and Right. Personally, I have no particular yen for either corporate capitalism or Marcusan Leninism, still less for the New Right and its naive dogmatism. The standard by which I wish to be judged is: do I transcend the shortcomings of *both* Right and Left? Can I draw from each, without accepting either lock, stock and barrel?

# 10: Needs Must

How do needs provide us with imperatives? Where precisely does the imperative power of need lie? This chapter explores this crucial question.

## Means and Ends

If you think about it, it only makes sense to talk of needing something if you need it *for* some purpose. To say that I need a hammer, but that I don't need it *for* anything, really does not make sense. If I don't need the hammer for some purpose, then I simply don't need it.

Of course, there are lots of occasions where it would be silly to ask what something is needed for. I would not ask 'What for?' if you told me that 'She needs to eat', or 'The car needs new tyres', or 'I need a rest'. If I did, I'd be likely to get a punch on the nose or to lose friends rather quickly. The answer is obvious, and generally agreed, and to challenge it is to be pedantic and awkward.

There are many cases of need, however, where there is little consensus as to what a thing is needed for. In such cases, it would appear helpful to know at least what the thing is needed for; without clarity over goals, how can there possibly be sensible debate about means?

In practice, this clarification of ends rarely occurs. 'Men need work', 'Children need education' are axioms of our modern society; yet people rarely ask 'What for?', perhaps *because* of a niggling fear that there may be no consensus, and we would rather not have to face up to that. The effect of not considering goals is that the need—for education, work, sex, etc.—becomes an absolute. It ceases to be a means toward something, and becomes an end in itself. Nowhere is this more clearly seen than in the frequent reference to 'a man's need for work' during periods of high unemployment.

One consequence of this reluctance to examine ends and goals is that it becomes difficult or impossible to envisage alternative means to the goal. If the means is mistaken for the end, then it is not possible to consider whether there are better means. This can be an important factor in emotional depression. Consider the person who is depressed because there is no longer paid work for him or her. Having a job has ceased to be a means toward an income, creativity, fulfilment, joy, identity, reducing loneliness or whatever, and has become an end in itself. Alternative ways of getting by, of being creative or reducing loneliness cannot even begin to be considered. Having a paid job becomes a need which cannot be questioned. No amount of counselling that tries to show alternative ways of attaining the ultimate goal will succeed, because as far as the person is concerned the need, a job, *is* the ultimate goal.

Of course, many activities and relationships are not directed toward any goal. A friendship, for example, is not *for* anything. If it were, then the friend would be dispensable, a mere means to some end, and could be dropped when no longer required; clearly this would not be friendship. Likewise, having and rearing children is not generally *for* anything. It may not be possible to say what one's children need love for, but there is no doubt that it is good to love one's children, that parents *ought* to love their children, indeed that they have a *duty* to love their children. Saying that children need love is simply another way of saying that parents ought to love their children.

But there remains the question of why in this century talk of the duties of parents has been largely replaced by talk of the needs of children. Is it not because duties refer to a moral framework, and many people today would prefer to do without traditional morality? Do we not feel that needs refer to the objective facts of how things are, in this instance to the facts of the psychology of childhood? And are not facts a more acceptable basis for action today than old-fashioned morality? Let's explore this a little further.

## Needs Must

When needs becomes things in themselves, they become 'reified' (or thingified — from the Latin *res,* a thing). They then take on the character of imperatives. If there is no possibility of discussing a higher goal, and no possibility of alternatives, then there is no question but that the need should be met. Whether the need *can* be met is not at all certain, as the person without work is all too painfully aware, but that it *should* be met there is no doubt. What reification succeeds in doing is to make the need into an imperative. Without reference to values or goals, we imagine that the imperative derives from the need for a job, which is believed to be a fact.

One advantage of this is that it makes life more simple. Having excluded any discussion of values or of alternative means to attain our goal, we no longer have to think, to consider, to debate. Our life is governed by a set of facts — the need to work, the needs of children, the need for security, and so on. This is very attractive to us because we have to organize the complexity of human existence into something we can make sense of, and facts and things are what make sense to post-Enlightenment Western people. Unlike traditional African peoples, who find order and stability in personal relationships, we find relationships distinctly unstable and seek order in the objective world of things (or at least our men do, and men play a large part in telling us how to think).[1] And since the Enlightenment, we trust what we take to be facts more than we trust values; we trust science more than we trust God. A world apparently reduced to a set of factual, objective needs is a world we feel we can handle.

Although needs masquerade as indisputable facts, they are actually rather more elusive. For example, it is very difficult to assess, measure and compare health needs. How can a hospital administrator with limited resources for expansion put a figure on the need for more orthopaedic beds? How can a regional hospital administrator compare the need for more community-based nurses with the need for a sophisticated brain-scanner? How can a government compare the need for more higher education with the need for more hospitals? At root, needs do *not* make the world any simpler; perhaps the contrary.

However, needs have an uncanny knack of *appearing* to make the world simpler. Administrators and politicians know this only too well; they know that an effective way to gain public support is to tell the public of the need for a brain-scanner for the city, or of the country's need for more teachers. And when the public become aware of a single need like that, it seems imperative to them that the need be met. A good example is the way in which American wilderness preservationists like the Sierra Club introduced the notion of outdoor recreation as a need (rather than, say, as a minority — or even majority — preference), and gained massive public support as a result. 'We need Z' has an urgency and a moral claim that 'We want Z' does not have.

Needs provide justifications for individuals as well as for politicians. To say that I have a need for achievement implies that I *must* get on at work, otherwise something deep in me will not be fulfilled; which is more powerful than simply saying that I am ambitious, for many ambitious people may be thwarted without that destroying their inner soul. So to talk not of ambition but of a need for achievement brings in the connotation of necessity; even if there is no evidence that something inside will go twang if I don't get on up the career ladder, the very use of the word 'need' gives an urgency to my ambitions. From here, it is a very easy step to saying that the need *ought* to be met.

Once we have stablished a need, then all kinds of other things are supposed to follow: 'People *need* sex . . . therefore they have a *right* to it . . . therefore we can *want* it without condemnation'. It is not just advertisers who use this supposed logic, we all do. 'Children need love . . . therefore we ought to love them.' In everyday conversation, we all try to derive moral imperatives from a supposedly factual world of needs. It readily justifies otherwise contentious actions, as well as actions about which there is consensus.

The Western world has employed three bases for morality, three ultimate justifications for why we should behave in such-and-such a way. The first, heavily influenced by Judaism and Christianity, based ethics on a divinely revealed law. This was undermined between the sixteenth and eighteenth centuries, partly because of the Protestants' insistence that the divine law was given as much to reveal human incapacity as to be obeyed. God's grace replaced the law as the basis of Christianity.

But people still believed in moral dos and don'ts, the legacy of centuries of legalistic Christianity. So, many people came to believe in the autonomy of morality. Morality is self-evident, they asserted. It is obvious how people ought to behave one to another, if only they will listen to their consciences. You can derive an 'ought' only from other 'oughts', and morality is a self-contained system. This view found expression in the American Declaration of Rights.

The trouble with this approach was that it provided no

court of appeal should someone dispute the obviousness of a moral command. If you could no longer appeal to divine command, what could you appeal to? Increasingly, philosophers noted that people were appealing to the facts, to statements about the nature of a thing, to how a thing *is*. To give an example, the nineteenth century utilitarians justified an action in terms of its factual consequences, notably whether it produced pleasure or pain. This then is the third basis for morality, a naturalistic basis. Morals, if we are to have morals, are justified in terms of what we know of human nature and the nature of society, in terms of the findings of psychology, economics and sociology.

Yet this clearly entails problems too, for consequences are by no means always predictable, and social scientists are notoriously in disagreement about the nature of persons, societies and economies. How, for example, may a utilitarian judge whether a particular consequence is painful or pleasurable? The judgement may well depend on people's moral beliefs. Certainly whether people find pornography pleasurable or painful depends on their moral beliefs.

It is within this third tradition that the everyday use of 'need' falls. Need enables us to 'perceive' imperatives in the world of facts.

But *do* people get moral imperatives from a factual world of needs? I do not think this happens at all, though we find great comfort in thinking this is what is happening, for it confirms the humanistic/scientific/religionless spirit of the age. No, needs are not pure facts at all; they have values written deep into them. Needs make sense only by reference to some higher purpose, about which moral questions can always be asked. 'Human beings need to eat.' To what end? 'So that they do not starve.' You cannot deduce that humans ought to eat unless you introduce the judgement that human life is of value. Human beings ought to eat not just because of their need for food, but also because we value human life. So we are not deriving an *ought* from a factual *is,* but from a *value,* the sanctity of human life. The *ought* comes from a need that is ridden through with a value judgement.[2]

A clear example may be found in those who tie the notion of need to a philosophy of self-realization in which people are exhorted to meet their various needs and thus fulfil their potential. But we have many potentials, to be tyrants as well as democrats, sinners as well as saints; we have many needs, to be aggressive as well as to care, to survive personally as well as to love others. The question is: *which* needs, *which* potentials are desirable? This brings the whole philosophy of self-realization back to a very traditional morality: how do we want human beings to behave? You cannot get a programme for living out of objective facts alone.

## Me and the World

The imperative power of need rests not only on needs masquerading as unalloyed facts, but also on something else equally important.

Compare again the traditional motive of ambition with its modern equivalent, the individual's need for achievement. We have already noted the imperative power of the need for achievement over traditional ambition. There is another difference. One may be ambitious for selfish purposes, but altruistic acts can also be motivated by ambition: the missionary whose ambition was to convert China; the doctor whose ambition was to conquer malaria; the politician whose ambition was to abolish poverty. The reference point for ambition can be either the self, or some project outside of the self. But the reference point for the need for achievement can only be the self. The person with a need for achievement can only use the world for his or her own ends.

So, need often brings two powerful themes together: the theme of objectivity, facts, nature, necessity; and the theme of the centrality of the self. Note that the two are brought together not by logic, but by proximity, by association.

This is actually a quite staggering achievement. The whole of modern thought in the last two hundred years has been plagued by an apparently unbridgeable gulf between two of the main idols of modern civilization: the Individual, the centre of the universe; and the objective world of things as discovered by Science. How to reconcile the two? How to value the individual without making everything relative and subjective? How to reconcile subjective experience and objective reality? How to reconcile the freedom of the individual, with the view of science that our actions are determined, pre-programmed? While the philosophers and the intellectuals wrestle over this knotty problem, ordinary people have for practical purposes solved it in their own lives, simply by seeing themselves as in need. Need provides a view of *the self* that is believed to be *objective;* by replacing desire with need, the conflict between the pleasure principle and the reality principle is abolished at a stroke. Here is a way of talking about oneself that is objective; never again will one be accused of being subjective. Without ever having heard the word 'determinism', millions of ordinary people embrace it when they say 'Women need to have children', 'Men need work', 'Human beings need to actualize themselves'; and they embrace too another word they may not have heard of, 'individualism'. And by embracing both together, they bring together what philosophy has failed to bring together.

So, to question need is to open a whole Pandora's box of philosophical problems. This, then is the power of need: it shores up reality against all the contradictions of modern scientific, religionless humanism. *That* is why we welcome being in need. *That* is what is in it for us. By being in need, we can live seemingly protected from the contradictions of modern existence. If an anthropologist from Mars descended to examine the structure of everyday life in modern Britain or America, he would surely identify need as a central concept by which people order and make sense of their world.

Life as the project of meeting our own and others' needs, then, draws on two of the most powerful creations of the modern age, the individual and science. It makes both the self and objective reality central. How does it do this? By boldly saying they are one and the same thing. It enables modern people both to have their cake and eat it; they can have both the Individual and Objectivity.

If one of the problems of individualism is how to reconcile the freedom of the individual with the pre-programmed world revealed by science, another is how to reconcile individual freedom with the demands of society. Need is a magic potion that evaporates this problem too, or so it appears. Whereas previous eras saw the desires and needs of the individual as in perpetual tension with social norms and with the stability of society, the modern concept of need is so unequivocal about the centrality of the needs of the individual that society is reduced to a handmaid of these needs. There is no inherent tension.

Contrast Freud and Maslow on aggression and you can see the difference. Freud was quite old-fashioned; like traditional

Christianity, he saw aggression as innate, and in a constant and healthy tension with the social order. Maslow considers aggression an unfortunate and avoidable result of the frustration of basic needs; if society, in the form of the child's parents and teachers, were doing its job properly and not frustrating some of the child's basic needs, then there would be no aggression.

There is another way in which need resolves the individual/society conflict. By constantly diverting attention away from goals, ends and values, it hides the very real lack of consensus in modern, plural societies. Several examples of this have been given in Part One, so I do not have to expand on this here. What is common to all the examples is that dissensus in society, between marital partners, or between teacher and parent, evaporates in the mist of need, to be replaced by the supposedly objective necessities of the situation.

So need enables me, subjectivity personified, to live with objective reality, both the objective reality of the physical world and the objective reality of the social world. It enables *me* to live in *the world,* which is no mean achievement because, like every human being, I must know where I fit into the cosmos. It enables me to feel at home in a modern universe composed of facts, causes, things, and social constraints. This is no mere concern of philosophers; it is crucial for every man and woman if we are to be at ease in the world, if we are to have enough basic contentment to get through life.

The modern individual is supposed to take responsibility for his or her own life, to be in control of his or her destiny, at least according to the dogma of individualism. This causes a problem for most of us: on the one hand we support this dogma; on the other, we cannot stand the awful loneliness and responsibility this casts upon us. So what do we do? We make choices on our own, and then hide behind a rhetoric of need in order to avoid responsibility for the choice. The American general in Vietnam says it is *necessary* to bomb such and such a village, not that—in the light of the various alternatives—he has chosen to. The husband says that the car needs washing, not that he can't stand another hour of the yelling infant and that he has decided to dump the problem onto his wife and go out. Just as, in the days of Christendom, the Church justified social institutions and the actions of the powerful by baptizing them with the blessing of the Church, so today we baptize our choices under the name of need, and they become equally unquestionable. And, as in medieval times, the naked individual is thereby related to the structure of the universe. But this time, it is not to the universe God created, but to the set of necessary causations that science tells us is the universe. Need removes the fear of freedom from us as effectually as did the will of God for people in medieval times.

Need resolves several of the problems of modern existence. Nevertheless, it is itself a peculiarly modern notion, in particular in its starting and ending with the human being, and this is part of its attractiveness and power. It may cut at one stroke through several of the problems that have ensued from the Enlightenment, but that it is itself a child of the Enlightenment there is no doubt.

In order to see this, it is worth doing what Marx and Fromm and Maslow have also done: to contrast the modern view of need with the view of traditional Christianity. This, I believe, will highlight the attraction of needs to twentieth-century, religionless human beings.

**Christianity and Need**
Christianity starts with a God who does not need. The Holy Trinity is portrayed as self-sufficient, creating the universe as an act of love. (Contrast Hegel, for whom God needs to create the universe, needs to externalize himself, if he is to know himself.) The Judaeo-Christian God creates bountifully, and he creates a world that is lacking nothing, represented in the Genesis story by a garden of plenty, the Garden of Eden.

Needs, lacks and unfulfilled desires are portrayed as a result of the fall. Free exploration of God's garden is transformed by Adam and Eve into the need to toil and sweat and work if they are to survive. Their joy of knowing each other in sex is transformed by them into passion and desire. In Genesis, chapter 4, Cain, wandering aimless and lost after the murder of his brother Abel, starts a family because it is the only way he can defeat death and begin to start a life of his own, having rejected the life of fullness provided by the Creator. He needs to have a family. And he needs to build a city in order to provide shelter and continue his name. So, the early chapters of the Bible describe a world of need, but this need is not given by God, it is not the starting point, it is not inherent in the human condition. Rather, needs are created by human beings. Activities like work, sex and family life which God intended to be free responses to his bounteous creation quickly become transformed into necessities. This biblical view takes human need very seriously, but does not accept it uncritically; and the image of paradise, the Garden of Eden, is not a place where all our needs are met, but a state of existence in which needs do not arise.

God's project of salvation involves restoring this state. It involves turning us from seeing only our needs and how we best can meet them, and refocusing our eyes on the Creator and the richness of his creation. The account of heaven in the book of Revelation is one in which all eyes are on God rather than on ourselves, man. We are saved not by meeting our own needs and pulling ourselves up by our bootstraps, but by accepting the love and forgiveness of God: human need is very real, and repentance indispensable, but the *focus* is the grace of God, not human sin.

On those occasions in history when Christianity has made an important contribution to industry, science, politics or the affairs of the world, it has been because believers have understood the richness of God's creation and have gone freely into that world to explore and develop it. This, for example, seems to be agreed by historians to have been the contribution of the Puritans to industry and science. This is very different from seeing industry and politics as the process by which human beings pick themselves up off the floor to meet their own needs; it is activity inspired by the richness of God's world, not by the needs of human beings. This sort of free activity in the world is not possible once it has been decided that God is dead. All that is then left is man, or rather Man, who then fills the vacuum and becomes the star of the show.

There are occasions when Christian ethics makes human need the centre in a limited sense. St Paul, for example, saw marriage as instituted to meet the physical needs of men and women. Unlike modern romantics who glorify our sexual needs, Paul simply saw them as physical needs. They were inherently mundane, not heavenly, features of human beings, and institutions had to be devised to cater for them. So Christianity does not deny that humans have needs; it simply treats them for what they are. But the direction of life is to be found somewhere else.

## Humanism and Need

Once God is dismissed from the picture, as has been fashionable for at least two hundred years, what is left? Man. In my understanding, humanism is the view which sees human beings as all that matters. And, being intelligent, we humans are all too aware that our lives are dominated by needs, lacks, wants and desires. We can hardly deny this. We know that we are not autonomous and self-sufficient, we know that we have to act and work and love and play if we are going to fulfil ourselves. So meeting our needs, making up for our lacks, becomes the human project. This is progress. This is the Enlightenment vision of human life: humans desiring to be full and fulfilled, but having to create this for themselves out of an original state of need and lack. For some, this means the individual striving to meet his or her own needs (as in Hume, Maslow, Fromm); for others, it means that society is a system in which human needs are met (as in Hegel, and as in Talcott Parsons, an American sociological guru of the 1950s).

The key difference between Christianity and humanism arises with the question of whether human beings are alone in the universe. In Christianity, we are not. We look beyond ourselves to the Creator who sustains us, and this is reflected in social institutions. Marriage, for example, is seen as a reflection between human beings of the love which pre-existed them. God was love before we humans came along.

This is why the doctrine of the Trinity is central to Christianity: there has to be more than one person in the Godhead for God to be love, because love has to have a beloved as well as a lover. Without the Trinity, God would have needed people in order to love, and Christianity has always seen this as heresy. This pattern is reflected in society, where the love between parents pre-exists the birth of the baby. Babies are born into a world in which love already exists.

But in humanism, love is something which people have to create *ex nihilo* for themselves if they are not to tear themselves apart. Modern psychology focuses on the child and its need for love, rather than on the parents and their pre-existing love. Indeed, some modern psychology sees parents not as creating a loving environment at all, but as objects of hate, jealousy and frustration for the child; somehow the child's personality has to unfold of itself in a loveless world.

The modern nuclear family of Mum, Dad and two children, cut off from society in its cosy suburban home, is a good reflection of humanity trying to go it alone. And on what does this family focus its attention? The needs of the marital partners and of the child. Child rearing is seen as meeting the needs of children, not as directing them outwards to the wider world, preparing them for it and imparting its values. It is as if we are all sick patients in a hospital, and simply looking after each other takes up all of our collective time. This describes the humanist vision not only of mankind in general, but also of specific social institutions such as marriage, the family, work, politics, and even—in much modern Christianity influenced by humanism—the Church.

So humanism claims we are alone in the universe, and that God is a projection of human minds and human needs. Christianity claims that we are not alone, and that humanism grossly restricts our horizons and our experience by focusing on human beings and their needs.

Humanism prides itself on being optimistic about human beings. It criticizes Christianity for despairing of them as worthless sinners who have not the resources to rescue themselves but have to be picked up off the floor by a paternalistic God. As well as claiming to be optimistic, many humanists have also been very aware of the lacks/deficits/needs with which we are born. How then to reconcile optimism with our inherent neediness? The answer is simple: to see needs as good things. Humanism glorifies the very needs that Christianity saw as our prime flaw. It welcomes as a natural fact the mess that Christianity believes we got ourselves into.

When the meeting of human needs becomes the human project, the highest goal to which a person can dedicate himself, then it becomes terrifyingly easy to create ever more needs and to sell them as contributing to personal or social progress. If in meeting need we become autonomous, and if becoming autonomous is what becoming human is all about, then the more needs the better. This humanist view of need is tailor-made for late capitalism that must sell goods and services to all and sundry. The critics who see need as ideology are correct; but it is far from easy to rid ourselves of it, because it is deeply rooted in the very same humanist assumptions that the critics themselves hold.

(Christian views, of course, have also served as ideology. The Christian notion of self-denial, of self-sacrifice in the service of higher ideals, was well suited to early capitalism, which required people to save and be thrifty, to work hard and long, and not to be greedy for quick reward. Early capitalism required investment to get the production process going. Late capitalism requires mass consumption in order to keep production going.)

Humanism attempts to discard God and religion. But has it succeeded? Clearly there *are* basic deficits/lacks/needs with which we are born and which must be met; nobody can deny that. But to make this the basis of social existence, to make the meeting of need the process by which we become human, is to invent a system that is almost religious in the way it includes every human activity under a rubric that is far from provable. It is also like a religion in the dogmatic way that it excludes alternative ways of looking at life; in its view, personality development is nothing but the meeting of personal needs, the economy is nothing but the meeting (or exploiting) of needs, marriage is nothing but the mutual meeting of needs. It is a view that is metaphysical in that it is not provable, but is in addition deceitful in that it pretends to be otherwise. Need is the religion of the religionless, the morality of those who pride themselves on having progressed beyond morality.

# 11: The Price of Need

In Part One, we frequently came across problems that follow in the wake of seeing ourselves as bundles of needs. And in the previous chapter, I have hinted that the notion of the human project as the progressive meeting of human needs, though powerful and persuasive for contemporary people, is not the only way human beings have conceived of themselves. In this chapter I want to list a little more systematically the problems, and then in the final two chapters explore the possibility of liberation from seeing ourselves as bundles of needs.

## Dishonesty

As we have seen in the last chapter, the claim that needs are objective facts from which imperatives for action may be obtained is a lie. It is indeed a fact that I need water to live, but this fact is only of any importance because I value my life or because human beings in general value human life. To say that I should be given a drink of water follows ultimately not from my need for it, but from your valuing my life. Needs alone cannot give rise to imperatives, yet this is what virtually everyone has come to believe.

It is quite permissible to produce a hierarchy of needs that must be satisfied if humans are to be human, so long as it is recognized that this is metaphysics and not science. But the trouble with needs is that their very association with necessity gives the impression that needs are not arbitary, but rooted in nature, biology, science, and facts. As Patricia Springborg complains of the needs propounded by existential psychologists, 'The use of the term is strictly rhetorical, and they trade off the association of need with necessity to impress their readers that their normative recommendations are incontrovertible.'[1]

Such needs—metaphysics dressed up as incontrovertible facts—are often the property of powerful professional groups, such as psychiatrists. An incontrovertible fact in the hands of a prestigious expert leaves the client very little chance to dispute about 'needs'. The arrogance of some of these experts is illustrated by Maslow's claim to have demonstrated 'the possibility that a scientist could study and describe normality in the sense of excellence, perfection, ideal health, the fulfilment of human possibilities'.[2]

Woe betide us if we delegate to scientists the right to pontificate on the ideal human being. If they claim to so pontificate *as scientists,* then they are being dishonest and we are being fooled.

### Egocentricity

If needs gain part of their imperative force from our contemporary veneration of facts, they gain further force from our veneration of the individual. True not all needs refer to the individual, for example 'the nation needs more hospitals'. But there is a marked tendency in Western democracies for needs to refer to individuals rather than to larger social groups.

Work, for example, may be seen in some totalitarian countries as something the nation needs if it is to become economically powerful; in communist philosophy, work is the means by which the masses gain collective pride and power; Christianity has tended to view work as for the glory of God and in the service of others; but in contemporary Britain and America work is defined more with reference to the individual who is believed to need work in order to make a living and gain respect and self-respect.

Likewise motherhood, which in the Soviet Union is a glorious service rendered to the motherland, and which in many societies is a duty to the family line, in our society is a need, an instinct, or at least a desire on the part of the individual woman. Of course, work and motherhood and other needs may be justified in our society by purposes beyond the individual. For example, 'the nation needs to work to be economically strong in order to stand up to the Soviets'. But it is typical of modern democracies that the individual is the main reference point for needs.

If the needs of each individual are paramount, then each individual becomes an island. As we have seen in our consideration of marriage, child-rearing and social work, my needs are likely to conflict with yours. Seeing the meeting of the individual's needs as the main purpose of human existence is hardly likely to resolve such conflict. (By contrast, a framework which gave supreme importance to God, the community, the proletariat or the tribe would provide norms and rules and ethics by which such conflicts can be resolved.) Instead, people try to resolve such conflicts by attempting to determine whose need is the greatest; but this too is doomed to failure, because there is no way you can put the needs of one island on the same scale as the needs of another island.

Unless, that is, you communally adopt some hierarchy of universal human needs, as with Maslow and the basic needs economists of the United Nations. But two points have to be made about such hierarchies. One is that they can only be agreed upon by reference to some set of values common either to one society or to the whole human race. So as soon as you talk of hierarchies of need, you are moving away from the individual as reference point and moving back to much more traditional notions of what a community can together agree are its joint ideals; in fact, the desires of the community have replaced the needs of the individual.

The second point is that hardly anybody ever resolves a moral dilemma by reference to one of these hierarchies. It is clear that the need for food and clothing is more basic than the need for education, yet if there is a choice between giving money to the starving children of the world and paying for my own child's education, I—like the rest of us—will put my child's education first. Further, some of the most clearly moral actions in human history have involved reversing such hierarchies: Gandhi put freedom before personal survival, hunger strikers put their cause before their need for food.

Maslow, for one, would object to what I have said. He claims that the highest need, for self-actualization, is not self-centred, and that the self-actualized people he studied were marked more by their altruism than by their egocentricity. But that surely confirms what I am saying. Maslow, like myself, looks forward to living freely rather than out of need; he looks forward to being able to live without seeing every activity as a struggle to make up for some personal deficit. He laments that 'for many people the *only* definition of the meaningful life that they can think of is to be lacking something essential and to be striving for it'. Maslow's self-actualizers demonstrate that 'the ordinary, widespread philosophy of a meaningful life is a mistaken one, or at least an immature one'.[3] These self-actualized people are not motivated by the ordinary need to meet one deficiency after another, so Maslow invents a new term to cover them — 'growth needs'. But growth needs do not really have the character of needs at all. What Maslow actually succeeds in showing is that creativity and altruism are characteristic of people who have got beyond seeing life as a project of meeting needs; conversely, need-meeting and self-centredness go together. Which is exactly my point. Maslow's vision of a free, need-less person is actually rather similar to mine, but he is so hooked on the terminology of need that he describes even this state of non-need as a need!

Maslow demonstrates the egocentricity of needs in one further way. Though his self-actualizers tended to be altruistic, Maslow's psychology has gained wide popularity because it appears, at a loose reading, to be a justification for self-centredness. Most of his followers do see self-actualization as a need, the culmination of a personal quest for self-fulfilment, rather than as service to others. By insisting on retaining the language of need, Maslow has laid himself wide open to this kind of misunderstanding. This demonstrates the difficulty, once you start with uncritical acceptance of the validity of human needs, of ever escaping from being in need. Once you start using the language of need, even altruism appears to be a response to a personal search. By not being concerned with the self you will find yourself, is the lesson taught not only by Jesus but also by Maslow's self-actualizers; your self is one of those things that will never be found by seeking it. Yet that is not what people hear Maslow saying; they suppose him to be saying that self-actualization is the culmination of a personal search for the self. It is virtually impossible to use the language of need without implicitly justifying an egocentric view of oneself, and Maslow's apparent failure to understand this is why he is so persistently misquoted.

'What is wrong with being egocentric?' ask those who believe in putting their own needs first. Surely it is only when you have met your own needs that you can reach out to anybody else? Christopher Lasch has shown that, even if you do not object to self-centredness on moral grounds, it tends to produce loneliness for the individual, disconnection of one person from another, and furthers the fragmentation of society (in sociological jargon, the anomie). Concentration on the self's needs does not solve the problem of fragmentation, but worsens it. The United States is perhaps the most individualist society the world has ever known, with individuals isolated in a heartless, competitive economy, compounded of late by the heartlessness of bureaucracy. The response of many is to abandon society and to concentrate on their own needs; if other people bug you, then forget about the old morality of trying to please them. Each looks out for his or her own interests. But over the past century this is precisely what has created the fragmented, anomic society of today. So the response of attending to one's own needs is not the solution to the problem; it *is* the problem. It attempts to solve the problems of individualism by asserting individualism even more strongly.

Arising out of a pervasive dissatisfaction with the quality of personal relations, it advises people not to make too large an investment in love and friendship, to avoid excessive dependence on others, and to live for the moment — the very conditions that created the crisis of personal relations in the . rst place.

Concentrating on your own needs brings into your private life the very same ruthless survival of the fittest ethos that characterizes the public world of American capitalism: 'When personal relations are conducted with no other object than psychic survival . . . private life takes on the very qualities of the anarchic social order from which it is supposed to provide a refuge.' Personal life is devastated by the very same thing that has devastated society.[4]

Perhaps the problem is not need itself, but the sorts of needs to which we address ourselves. In Britain and North America we are preoccupied with biological and psychological needs, as befits a culture obsessed with the centrality of the individual and revering science. In the Soviet Union, the needs of society are paramount. In Catholic communities, religious needs may take precedence. The problem in any one society arises when need is hitched to the cart of that society's ideals, for then it gives those ideals an aura of necessity and inevitability. To talk of the individual's needs makes it seem that the centrality of the individual is not a socio-political choice, but a necessity. To talk in the Soviet Union of society's needs makes the centrality of the Soviet state not an historical creation but a timeless necessity. A society that could talk of the individual's needs, society's needs, religious needs and perhaps yet other needs would certainly be a healthier and richer society than any we see now. However, I cannot envisage such a society ever existing, for need has a totalitarian effect: the individual will not allow that society has needs; society will not allow that the individual also has needs; in the concept of biological necessity, there is no place for spiritual needs; and so on. The very necessity of any one kind of need tends to exclude other kinds.

Some may object that even in our individualistic society, much human activity is devoted to meeting the needs of others rather than the needs of oneself, mothers and teachers caring for children's needs, lovers caring for each other, and so forth. Surely such activity is not egocentric?

I'm not so sure. 'You [the child, for example] need me [mother, teacher]' implies my status, my power over you, and your dependency on me. You are an isolated individual in need, and the only basis for your relation to me is that I am another individual with resources that can meet your need. 'You need me' highlights me, my gifts and my resources. I am still central. This is very different from certain alternative ways of conceiving our relation, for example, 'I have a duty to you', 'I have a responsibility to you', 'You are entitled to succour'. These alternatives refer ultimately not to your weakness and my strength, but to the community and its social order, or to religion and its moral order. It relates you and me to something beyond ourselves, and so the limelight comes off me and my gifts.

## Dependency
To have and to meet needs is fashionable; to be dependent is not. For some strange reason, the relation between the two—that one is dependent on those who meet, and even on those who define, our needs—is not usually perceived. There are far more critics of dependency than there are of need.

Ivan Illich is an exception. He wants a society in which people can once again define their own needs rather than learn what their needs are from self-appointed experts; people must relearn how to identify wants from experience, rather than be told what they need by professionals. He wants communities of lay people to determine their own needs together, a 'return to an era that fosters participatory politics in which needs are defined by general consent' rather than by a coterie of professionals and experts.[5]

But Illich does not want to abandon the concept of need. He wants us to be allowed to determine our own needs, not just—note—our own wants or desires. Is this possible? Is it possible to have needs without dependency? There seem to be several problems about this, which I would now like to explore. I must say straightaway that I want to discuss Illich at some length precisely because, more than anyone else, he has raised our awareness of how problematic it is to be in need. I am not convinced by his solution, but he is raising many of the right questions.

I am not at all sure that lay people can be the only, or ultimate, judges of their own needs as Illich wants. No doubt they are the best placed to know wants and desires, but needs refer to objective reality as well as to subjective experience, and there may be others with greater knowledge of the subject. If I say, 'I need a screwdriver to hit this nail into the wall,' I am referring to an objective reality, and am opening myself to someone replying, 'No you don't. You need a hammer.' Indeed, even if I say, 'I *want* a screwdriver to hit this nail into the wall', I am still opening myself to possible correction by someone who is more of an expert on nails and walls than I. To retort to his correction, 'Shut up, *I* decide what I need,' is the foolish reply of someone who lives in a private world unconnected to both reality and society.

If Illich is saying that ordinary folk have as much business discussing their needs as any expert, then that is fair enough. But this is a slippery slope, because the expert may have studied the facts of the matter and may well be more aware than us of what we need. It is very difficult to talk of one's own needs and yet maintain control of the discussion. To claim that a self-defined need is automatically better than one defined by experts assumes that either we have complete information (which often is clearly not the case) or that a decision made by oneself is inherently better than one made for us, however slim or even false the information on which it was made (which only makes sense if we are indeed the centre of the universe and everything else is relative to us). It may be replied that the function of the expert is simply to provide information so that individuals may make rational decisions for themselves. But this means that the expert is able to control the information and define what is relevant information, which is not far short of controlling the decision itself.

The individual may have all the relevant information and be aware of all the possibilities, but may not be sufficiently articulate. To have someone speak for the individual sounds fair enough at first, until one remembers that this is precisely what an advocate or barrister is supposed to be. What is to stop the spokesman from becoming an expert, on whom the person comes to be dependent?

Whichever way you turn, it seems that you end up on the slippery slope to reliance on some expert or other. What will save us from this? One possibility is to claim that as our basic needs are universal, natural and biological, the individual can decipher his or her own needs. But nature is never directly observed. Our most basic needs, such as for food and shelter, are experienced in even the most primitive of cultures through the eyes of that culture. A house is never just a roof and walls; it is home, the universe in microcosm, God's temple, or however else one thinks of it. Food is never just food; it is also sociability, caring, sharing, or whatever other meaning one's culture gives to meals. To claim that the individual can, by himself, see the necessities imposed by nature is to posit a Robinson Crusoe individual, and human beings simply are not like that. A *community* can interpret nature, indeed all communities do, but this is more accurately described as the community defining its own values rather than its needs.

Lastly, the danger of Illich's policy of enabling people to define their own needs is that they may come to believe that they are succeeding in this, when in fact there are severe limitations in the extent to which they can define their own needs. People will have ditched the old experts and, without realizing it, come to be manipulated by new, unproclaimed experts. Illich or Freire, out in the Brazilian jungle helping the natives to determine their own needs and their own fate, may end up as just such unproclaimed experts (something of which Illich himself is all too aware). Or a women's movement consciousness-raising group may pride itself on being able to discover what are women's real needs instead of being told what they are by (predominantly male) experts; but what inevitably happens to a greater or lesser extent is that they have taken their needs from the group's self-styled guru or from the latest feminist book they have read, or from some other self-effacing (and therefore dangerous) authority.

I do not want all this to pour cold water on liberation movements, consciousness-raising groups, and so on. They are struggling in the right direction, but I truly fear the coming of a world in which people believe they are autonomous, while all along their needs are being defined by others. Better to be in thrall to the experts and know it. There is real danger that conscientization will produce a world not unlike the very worst image of capitalism: a population that thinks it can choose for itself, but which is entirely manipulated by the public relations boys. All that will have changed is who is doing the PR on behalf of whom.

### Fragmentation

I tried to show in the chapter on welfare that seeing people as bundles of needs tends to go hand in hand with a fragmented view of the person. Each profession has been built up in order to meet a particular kind of need, and so each bit of the individual is parcelled out to a different profession. Attempts to reintegrate the person, such as the reorganization of social work in Great Britain, are likely to fail so long as they are dominated by the professional provider/needy client syndrome.

In her book *The Death and Life of Great American Cities,* Jane Jacobs has provided a nice example of how the generation of needs leads to a fragmented life.[6] Time was when children played in the street, and old men and housewives sat on the doorstep watching the varied life of the street; the children were safe because there were always friendly eyes on them. Then the city planners and highway authorities came to put the requirements of the automobile first; they reduced the width of sidewalks, which didn't help the vibrancy of street life. There was nowhere for the children to play, and if they did play in the street it was dangerous — not only because of the traffic, but because (without the ever-present eyes of adult acquaintances of their parents) they could easily get into trouble. So, a new need emerged: the need for play space, and special play areas were created, usually in parks. This divorced the child's play from the rest of city life, and children — not yet having been taught how to need — naturally responded by generally avoiding the parks and playgrounds.

Likewise with the city parks created by an earlier generation of planners who deemed slum dwellers to be in need of these little lungs of fresh air. Actually, the slum dwellers preferred the vibrancy of their street life (which is not to say they enjoyed the damp and cold and lack of facilities in their homes), and generally avoided the parks. For large chunks of the day, except when the affluent are out jogging or walking their dogs and later when mothers are out walking their prams, the parks are virtually deserted; so it is no surprise that most of New York's murders happen not in the slum streets, but in the very parks which were intended to meet the needs generated by the stress of city life.

I have argued in a previous book, *The Human Home*, that—with patterns of work so unbalanced that they generate a need for leisure in compensation—we have created a schizophrenic landscape, a landscape in two parts. There is the profane landscape of the industrial towns which few really care about; and there is the sacred landscape of national parks, preserved old towns and villages, which nobody is allowed to touch or change. There is the profane world of the street which nobody claims responsibility for; and there is the sacred little enclave of our own house and garden. Householders blame the planners for allowing ugly new office blocks and the authorities for not mending the roads; but they are infuriated when the same planners and authorities tell them they may not extend their houses or cut down trees on their property. Whereas the authorities should take total responsibility for the public mess, nobody welcomes them poking even half a finger into one's private life. Is it any wonder that our environment lacks coherence?

Our needs make us dependent on experts—the social worker, the national park manager, the city highway engineer—each of whom can see, and is paid to see, only one of our needs, only one part of the bundle of human existence. And so our society, our economy, our landscape become more and more disjointed and schizophrenic.

## Addiction

Those who talk of needing a new car or a new coat are usually those who already have a car or a coat; those who haven't, may talk of *wanting* one, but rarely of needing one. Those who talk of sexual needs are usually those who are or have been sexually active; those who have never had it rarely talk of sex as a need. Those who talk of the hills and wild places as a need, either for themselves or for urban humanity in general, are those who get out into the great outdoors quite regularly; the Harlem mother of six rarely expresses any desire for the great outdoors. The unemployed who talk of their need for work are those who have already had jobs; many nineteen-year-olds who have never had a job do not (indeed their elders who have or have had jobs are petrified lest a generation arises that does not need work).

This suggests that needs often arise *after* the good (a car, a coat) or the pleasure (sex, backpacking, work) has been obtained. The notion that we start off with needs which then get satisfied simply does not fit the facts. The fact is rather that we live in a world rich with possibilities which, once realized, become needs. We like them so much, we integrate them so well into our everyday life, that we conclude we cannot get by without them. We do not progress from necessity to freedom; all too often we regress from freedom to necessity.

The standard reply to this is, 'Ah, but the Peruvian peasant *does* need a coat/the forty-five-year-old spinster would be a lot happier if she had a sex life/the urban black *does* need to get out of the city/the nineteen-year-old *does* need a job—only they don't know it. They don't know the possibilities; their horizons are limited; they need education/conscientization.' Well, this is possible, but only if you place a higher authority on the self-styled expert who has experienced the good or the pleasure and who proclaims that all need it; only if you assume that the masses do not know what they need. Or rather, that those who have more are better informed about what people need than those who have less.

I see no reason as a general rule to assume this. The dispassionate outside observer, faced with an urban black who enjoys city life and a suburban white who can't stand it and believes everyone needs to get away to the great outdoors if they are to remain sane, is more likely to pity the suburban white for his discontent. Or, faced with a Cantonese worker who gets around on his bicycle at an average speed of ten miles per hour, and a Los Angeles executive who gets around in his Oldsmobile at an average speed (when you add into the equation the time taken to earn the money to pay for the car) of eight miles per hour, one may be forgiven some incredulity on hearing the executive say that he needs a car, or that he feels he must buy another one for his teenage son or daughter; and forgiven even more incredulity when one hears the suburban white or the executive tell the rest of the world what it needs.

## Frustration

People often look to necessity as a way of resolving conflict and providing guidelines.

I've never liked shopping, because I have terrible difficulty making the kinds of choices one has to make in shops; some years back, I attempted to resolve this by always asking 'Is this item really necessary?', and if it wasn't I wouldn't buy it. But as we have seen, necessity does not always succeed in getting us out of such conflicts. Our needs and those of others expand. Often it is not clear what something is necessary for, and trying to work that out sometimes resulted in increasing the emotional burden of my shopping. My needs and your needs may conflict. And so on.

The trouble with need as a method for resolving conflict is that, if it does not succeed, the resultant frustration is magnified. We can discipline ourselves to accept that not all our wants can be satisfied, indeed that was what bourgeois Victorian child-rearing was all about. But to have an unmet need, that is a crime against nature, and our generation worships nature. As Daniel Yankelovich found among those involved in a quest for self-fulfilment and who saw themselves as bundles of needs, 'They operate on the premise that emotional cravings are sacred objects and that it is a crime against nature to harbour an unfulfilled emotional need.'[7]

Frustration results not only from individual needs. Take a classic political conflict. I want more beds for my hospital; you want more teachers for your school; and there is not enough money to satisfy both of us. Or, environmentalists believe there is a need to keep the Colorado Rockies pristine and undeveloped; oil companies argue that the national economy needs more oil and that the oil shale in the Rockies must be extracted if that need is to be met. Each side convinces first themselves and then potential allies that they are indeed talking about needs, that there are no alternatives, that the desired end is sacred and unquestionable (the purity of the Earth/sustaining economic growth/reducing dependence on the Arabs or the Soviets). To talk of needs rather than strategies, policies, alternatives, possibilities, desires, or goods may increase your chances of gaining support and winning; but if in the end you lose, then rather than feel you've lost a political battle you feel you've lost a holy war, and so do your many supporters.

Fred Hirsch in his brilliant book, *Social Limits to Growth,* distinguishes material goods from positional goods. Hirsch defines these two terms in a special way in which 'material' goods—such as certain kinds of education—need not be actual physical objects. *Material goods* are valued things which conceivably all of us could have; we can, or could in a perfect world, all have clean air, fresh water, enough to eat, education as something valued for its own sake, a roof over our heads. *Positional goods* are those where our ability to possess the good depends on our possession of the good relative to other people's lack of it. Education as a means of social advancement is a positional good: not everybody can have a job at the top, so expanding educational provision will simply mean that you need more and more education to get to a job that your father could have got with less and your grandfather with less still. By contrast, education as a good in itself can be expanded indefinitely, and made available to more and more people. Or, whereas everyone can have a house, in even the most affluent society only a few could ever have the ideally situated house: in the countryside, without another house in sight, but with quick access to the city. Or, in a time of full employment, everyone can have a job, but—so long as jobs are arranged in a hierarchy of income and status—not everybody can have a good job.

Hirsch has shown that there is a tendency for modern economies to move from being dominated by material goods to positional goods. This is not inevitable (for example, there is no reason why education cannot be valued for its own sake), but it is likely. Material goods are relatively easy to produce, and once the demand for them has been satisfied, an ever-expanding economy (and I would add, an ever-expanding culture) tends to latch onto positional goods as the easiest way of expanding. And so do individuals. You take great pride in the first house of your very own (a material good); and then you yearn for a better situated house (a positional good).

The historical and personal tendency to shift from demanding material to positional goods that Hirsch has demonstrated is accompanied by, as I have tried to demonstrate, a shift from seeing goods as goods (that is, as good things, desirables, wants, blessings) to seeing them as needs. Put the two together, and you have a recipe for perpetual frustration. By definition, positional goods are denied to the many, and if in addition they are seen as needs then the many will be unhappy. A society and an economy based on *material goods* can be a reasonably content society; one based on *positional needs* will inevitably be unhappy. And people actually welcome their needs! Well, welcome material needs if you must ('I have a thirst for knowledge'), but woe betide us if we all welcome positional needs ('My son must get a good education if he is to get further in life than I did').

One final point about frustration. Many good things are not means to an end, nor ends in themselves (needs are always one or the other or both). Often good things are by-products. Happiness or contentment for example: you cannot aim for them, but they may result from other things. This is also true of self-realization, as Frankl has noted. The trouble with calling such things needs is that people then strive after them, and — like Hirsch's seekers after positional goods — they will most likely be disappointed.

That good things are often by-products is hinted at by those previous generations that called them 'blessings': a blessing is something that comes to you, perhaps unexpected; it cannot be striven after or grasped. Which is what Jesus meant when he said that those who gain their selves are those who are prepared to lose themselves.

A life or a society dominated by the meeting of need is a hard, harsh world, joyless and puritanical. One sees it in the lives of some of those seeking self-fulfilment, and in some societies preoccupied with meeting the basic needs of the people. Joy, though, cannot be sought. It is the result of serendipity, of happy chance. There may or may not be a need present, but that pales into insignificance in the presence of joy.

**Limitation**

We have seen how needs provide a structure to everyday life. The man does not have to question on a Monday morning why he is going out to his dead-end job because he knows he needs it, and his family need him to be the breadwinner; the wife need not question her voluntary imprisonment in the house, because she knows her child needs her. This comforting structure is effective because the needs rule out of court all alternatives: the wife does not have to choose from the wide range of systems of child care that are theoretically possible (though hardly available practically), because she knows her child needs her at home all to itself. It is precisely because needs limit our freedom of choice, limit our responsibility, that we welcome them. Indeed, a life in which every decision had to be made from a million alternatives would be intolerable: we must have some limitations if we are to remain sane. (Which is why I sometimes get near to insanity when shopping!)

But this limitation can go too far, and frequently does. Once everybody knows that men need employment, then the unemployed are doomed to misery (or to being rejected if they are not miserable); men who would have much to both give and gain by looking after their own children do not consider the possibility (still less do their wives); the workaholic whose wife has barely seen him in twenty years rejects the idea out of hand when a friend suggests he and the wife take a year off and go travelling together.

So we imprison ourselves, and we hand the keys over to those experts and pundits who continually tell us what we do and do not need. We reject the potential richness of human life, as though we could see only one colour of a rainbow. How can we liberate ourselves from this? *Can* we liberate ourselves?

# 12: Alternatives to Need

Is life a matter of religionless human beings having no other project than meeting their own and other's needs? I am certainly not the first to see the problems inherent in such a project; various alternatives have been proposed, and I will examine some of these in this chapter. If we are not to be in need, how else are we to see ourselves?

## Need as Part of a Bigger System

One alternative has been proposed by some who agree that there are major problems if you make meeting need *the* human project, but who wish to retain the notion of need. They say that need is terrible as the basis for a total philosophy or religion, but that *within* another philosophy or religion there is a place for need. As human beings we have to recognize certain necessities (gravity, for one), but that doesn't mean we have to say that the whole of life is governed by necessity. We may well have to start with ourselves and with our own needs, but from there we can go on to relate freely to others. They agree that the individualism inherent in many needs makes a poor basis for community, but that does not mean that the individual does not have needs.

This is a 'basic needs' approach. It says that you must start by ensuring that people have enough to eat and somewhere to live, and only then can they get on with being human; or you must provide for the basic emotional needs of the child, who otherwise will not grow into a responsible person able to make moral choices.

In theory, this sounds OK. But in practice it never quite works out that way. The needs keep breaking out of their appointed bounds and challenging the religion or philosophy that was supposed to be their master.

This may be seen in those churches that present Christ as the answer to all our needs, and never portray the Christian life as anything beyond this; so the congregation spends its time evangelizing and counselling those with personal problems, and there is no vision of the Christian life being anything other than a hospital in which needs are met. Such churches are rarely liberated to make positive Christian

141

contributions to art, politics, or the craft of housework; they have no vision of the world as a garden which we are called to explore and open up. And they may not cope when members experience pain and suffering.

If those with an explicit otherworldly view cannot get beyond their needs, is there any hope that the religionless humanist can? We have seen that basic needs never seem to have an end; as they are met, what had previously been thought of as luxuries (either material or emotional) get redefined as basic needs.

And how can the professions, those who have a stake in us having needs, be kept under check? The kind of church just referred to is a good example: the pastor has the task of ministering to people's needs, and he makes sure his congregation know that this is what the Christian life is really all about. He is not paid to be a Christian artist or politician, so such activities get shunted to the sidelines and probably out of view altogether. A church dominated by its pastors, ministers and priests has no more chance of escaping from need than a child dominated by its mother, a health service dominated by doctors, or an economy dominated by a mass-consumer market.

Then there is the problem of reification. Needs which, if you think about them, are means ('I need another car', 'You need to see a doctor') to some end (mobility, health) are regularly experienced not as means at all but as ends. To the thoughtful person, the means only make sense in reference to a higher end, which can only be determined by reference to values, which can only be determined with reference to one's faith or philosophy of life. But in practice, the means become the end, require no justification, and so escape from religion or philosophy.

### Rescuing Need by Reducing It

Many, from Marxists to *laissez-faire* liberals, understand how needs—or rather, they think, *some* needs—are socially constructed, and they propose some criterion for determining what valid needs are. Their critique of needs goes a long way, but always reserves some category of needs that are not only OK but which must very definitely be attended to. They want to rescue the notion of need by reducing it in some way or other.

1. One possibility is to claim that social needs are artificial and should not be seen as needs, whereas physical needs really are needs and must be attended to.

This entails considerable problems however. First, it discriminates against cultural needs, and thereby discounts most of what passes for civilization! F. A. Hayek states the problem:

> Innate wants are probably confined to food, shelter and sex. All the rest we learn to desire because we see others enjoying various things. To say that a desire is not important because it is not innate is to say that the whole cultural achievement of man is not important.[1]

Not only does this approach discount the cultural achievements of human beings, it also discounts the experience of those whose so-called basic physical needs are not met and who are often more concerned about culture and religion than about their physical needs. It discounts the fact that to have unmet physical needs is to suffer, and that suffering is bearable only if there is some purpose or meaning to it — and purpose and meaning are personal, cultural and religious, not physical. So to affirm the pre-eminence of the physical is to compound the suffering of those who lack some of their physical needs. I recall a radio talk given by the cellist Jacqueline du Pré, stricken by multiple sclerosis, entitled 'I Really Am a Very Lucky Person', in which she described both the joy and pleasure in music, and the love, which she had given and received. Though her physical infirmity has curtailed her musical performance, somehow what was uppermost in her experience was not her physical needs but decidedly non-physical blessings such as love and joy.

The policy implications of a view which takes only physical needs seriously are indeed spartan. Love and joy would not enter into it. Instead, this approach to need

> encourages us to regard the sphere of needs largely as a quantitive problem: each person needs a certain amount of nutrients, shelter, space, and social services. The practical outcome of this statement of basic needs is reflected in some of the social policies of the existing welfare state: bulk foodstuffs for the poor, the drab uniformity of public housing projects, and the stereotyped response of bureaucracies.[2]

143

It really is impossible to imagine a world in which people are considered only as biological creatures with nothing but physical needs, even if merely as a starting point.

It is unimaginable not only because it mistakes the nature of cultural or social needs and denigrates them, but also because it mistakes the nature of so-called physical needs. These are not so easily distinguishable from 'artificial' needs (as Professor Hayek seems to assume in the quote a little earlier). I have noted at several points in this book how even our physical needs for food and shelter are always experienced through cultural spectacles; when I'm hungry, I would hardly be pleased to be offered raw meat or frogs legs, though they would be just what would satisfy someone from prehistoric times or a contemporary Frenchman. A house is not just shelter; it is a home. Post-war rehousing policies that have defined housing standards in purely physical terms have produced vast deserts of concrete, some of which have already become slums.

So, it really does not get us very far to say that physical needs are universal and must be satisfied if people are to have any chance of being fully human, whereas social needs are not. One cannot say, for example, that work consists of two elements: a basic physical need to earn one's subsistence, plus a cultural norm that one works beyond what is necessary for physical subsistence. In practice, the motivation to work is not split up like this. When people lose the motivation to work (as happened with one of my friends who was off work for several months due to illness), they lose *all* motivation; they do not retain some basic need to earn their subsistence.

So far, my objection to distinguishing basic physical needs from 'unnecessary' cultural needs has been theoretical. But it leads to a very practical problem: it is very difficult working out what *are* basic physical needs and what levels of satisfaction would meet those needs. Perusal of any attempt to make such judgements will quickly reveal the conflicts and contradictions with which the attempt is riddled.

2. There is another way of trying to rescue the notion of need, similar to restricting it to physical needs. This is to distinguish real from false needs, natural needs from artificial needs. But this is even more fraught with problems than the attempt to discover our basic physical needs. People have never been

agreed as to what counts as 'natural', and who is to say what is a real need and what a false one? The only way you can do this is by reference to some ultimate set of values: for example, a self-defined need may be considered real, whereas one created by advertising may be considered artificial, but that is only possible because of certain basic beliefs about the value of individual autonomy and choice. What is basic is not needs at all, but values.

3. A third way of rescuing need is to restrict it to valid uses, to say that only self-defined needs are permissible. Illich's attempt to do this has been discussed in the previous chapter. Though it has some admirable practical outcomes, we saw that it really does not overcome the problem of need.

4. A fourth strategy is to distinguish general from specific needs. Raymond Plant argues that there are some basic needs which are not dependent on moral values.[3] Rather, they are prerequisites without which people cannot be moral agents: they are, *survival* and *autonomy*. In any culture, without these needs being met, people cannot act responsibly; as needs, they are not dependent on any particular moral code for people to agree that they are needs. More particularly, for autonomy three hindrances must be removed: arbitary power, ill-health, and ignorance; the removal of these may therefore be described as universal human needs.

This is an admirable attempt, for it does understand that most so-called basic needs are actually rooted not in the human condition itself but in values that some human beings have chosen and others have rejected. But I'm not sure how far Professor Plant's programme gets us:
(a) His universal needs are so general that they do not seem to have many specific implications for actual people and actual societies. As I have shown, people look to needs not as an abstract philosophy, but in order to know what to do and in order to have motives and rationalizations for what they do. Just as they use their physical needs to account for their cultural preferences ('I'd feel naked in a kilt'), so they will draw all kinds of illicit and more specific needs from the basic needs for survival and autonomy.
(b) There is also the objection that, as a matter of historical fact, some of humanity's finest moral agents — Jesus Christ,

for instance — were hardly granted autonomy by their political context; certainly Jesus was subject to arbitary power (admittedly not so arbitary as in some political systems, but the Roman administration in Israel in his time would fail most present-day criteria for guaranteeing the citizen's basic right to autonomy). Gandhi suffered ill-health as a result of his political tactics, but did that make him any less of a moral agent? Certainly to say that physical health is a prerequisite for moral decisions is to question the validity of the last wishes of many dying people; it means that patients have no right to determine what kind of health care they get; it means all those martyrdoms that were preceeded by pain and suffering must be discounted because the martyr did not know what he was doing when offering up his life. I would not deny that ill-health does provide a hindrance to clear moral thinking (what doesn't?) or that we may make some allowance for 'he grumpy old man because he's had to live with one internal ache and pain after another for longer than some of us have been alive. Certainly good health is a good thing, but is it *necessary* for responsible decision making? Jesus, Gandhi and millions of others indicate otherwise.

If autonomy were widely regarded as a necessary prere-quisite for decision making, it would be all too easy for some people to say, 'Well, I'm not granted autonomy by the government of my country, therefore I'm entitled to use brute force to change the system, without any moral qualms. Only when we have a free political system can we act as moral agents. Until then, it's the law of the jungle.' And it gives the old man with a liver complaint an excuse not to be caring or considerate.

So I fully agree that survival, autonomy, health, knowledge are good things, which I would want to see all men and women have as much of as possible, but it confuses the issue to call them needs.

## Bradshaw's Solution

Another alternative has been proposed in a much quoted article by Jonathan Bradshaw.[4] He notes that there are more demands on welfare services than can be met, so how is one to find a criterion of need that really ensures that the priority cases get dealt with? He notes that, in practice, four different things are meant by 'need' in welfare services: normative need (what the expert lays down as a need according to some professionally determined standard); felt need (what the client or customer wants); expressed need (those wants that the client actually makes known); and comparative need (how the clients in one area fare for welfare services compared with another area). Bradshaw wisely refuses to say which of these is 'real' need. Instead, he argues that for practical purposes those clients should be taken seriously who score heavily on all four counts; we may not know what need *really* is, but there is little doubt that such people certainly *are* in need. Once they have been catered for, an agency can look at those who score on only three counts, and so on.

This is an intelligent solution and, though complicated in practice, does bring to light the various value judgements underlying the different types of need. But we live in a society that is adept at creating needs, many of which are dubious on all kinds of grounds yet would pass all four of Bradshaw's criteria.

Take my need for a washing machine. The experts (advertisers) authoritatively tell me I need it; I believe I need it; I make my want known by being prepared to pay for it; and single men are seriously under-represented among washing machine owners, so here is a market of under-met need. Yet there are surely still grounds for questioning whether a single person like me does need a washing machine — the person in question has not much money, even less washing, plenty of spare time, could do with the exercise of bending and scrubbing, and in any case has nowhere to put the infernal machine.

Similar examples can be given from the field of welfare, which is what Bradshaw is concerned about. Certainly the need of the old and infirm for personalized transport meets all four criteria in a society such as ours where the spread of car ownership has led to the demise of public transport, of local stores, and of many neighbourly relations. Or the need for heroin of an addict could well count on all four grounds. But surely what is most important for social policy, and that is what concerns Bradshaw, is to create a society in which such needs do not arise. Certainly there must be first aid for those who have become immobile or addicted, which is what much social welfare is (rightly) all about, but without some means of criticizing the generation of need we will never liberate ourselves from need. Bradshaw enables us to sort our needs into some kind of order of priority, but goes nowhere toward liberating us from a life in need.

## Wants

Personal needs are an attempt to bring together objective reality and the prime importance of me to myself. Many of the problems concerned with attempts to rescue the notion of need have to do with the difficulty of grasping the objective aspect of a need — what *is* a physical need, a real need? How do you disentangle needs from values? Can you disentangle them from values? I concluded that you cannot.

So perhaps a better approach is to abandon altogether the concept of need and its connotations of objectivity? Abandon necessity and opt for freedom. Admit that all that we can know is the individual's wants and desires. We may disagree for ever over what Joe needs, but he knows what he wants. Nobody can tell him what he wants; in this there is one authority — Joe. There may, of course, be conflict between his wants and ours, and we will have to resolve that through the market (who can pay the most?), through the law (do Joe's wants harm another person?), or through politics (voting for the party that will do what we want rather than what Joe wants).

This is what may be termed the liberal alternative, and it gains considerable support in all Western countries. For centuries, our economies have been run in large part according to the principles of the free market, and some believe that *all* social relations should be conducted as though all life were a market. Joe determines his own wants, and in so far as he can pay, he should receive what he wants. This liberal mode of thinking has seen something of a renaissance since the 1970s.

For example, wilderness preservation groups in the United States had for years argued that wilderness was sacred, an important need of all Americans; they refused to enter into cost-benefit analysis of the merits of wilderness preservation *vis-à-vis* other uses of a particular piece of land, for this was to admit that wilderness was something less than an absolute need that had to be met at any cost. This won them some victories, but then in the late 1970s they began to realize that cost-benefit analysis could be persuasive. They costed

148

wilderness as a good for which people were prepared to pay, and more than once came up with the (to them) useful conclusion that, if people's purses represent their preferences, then they often prefer wilderness to oil or uranium. This was to shift the argument from wilderness being what Americans need to wilderness as what Americans want. Certainly this looked more democratic and escaped the earlier charge of an environmental élite telling the masses what they need.

There is a parallel shift in slogans to do with childbirth. In the 1950s the belief that women need to bear children in order to fulfil themselves was in its heyday. In the 1970s, the pro-abortion lobby in Britain used as its slogan, 'A Woman's Right to Choose'—the belief being that some women wanted to have children and some did not, and it was up to them to choose. Women were fed up with other people (male doctors, social workers and priests) telling them what they needed. So, needs were rejected in favour of wants, choices and rights. Of course, the battle still rages, and the hub of the fighting is over whether the woman is an autonomous individual, free to choose; or whether she has responsibilities to the unborn child, lives in an objective world about which others have knowledge as well as she, and is responsible to a moral code that existed prior to her own personal existence.

Resistance to basing welfare and other services on wants rather than needs comes from those who do not operate according to the market, or are critical of the market mechanism. For example, the idea that welfare services should be consumer-directed and should respond to the expressed demands of clients (as in private medicine and in a voucher system of education) is usually resisted by the paternalistic bureaucracies that currently run welfare services; by dedicated professional workers who see that a consumer-run system would not protect weak, inarticulate or ignorant people who do not know or cannot express their wants; and by Marxist intellectuals who argue that people in our present society are not free to know their own wants (though for some reason they do grant that even in our sexist, capitalist society women do know their own wants when they demand an abortion). Bureaucracies, monopolistic professions and Marxist intellectuals all correctly perceive that not all needs, and not even all wants, can be met by pure market forces.

In the liberal conceptual armoury, *rights* have an important place. A right, unlike a need, may be taken up or not, thus giving the individual choice and control. However, Illich has correctly pointed out that rights are usually rights to commodities or to professional services — the right to education, the right to health care, the right to decent housing, the right to a lawyer, and so on. You never hear talk of a right to think for yourself or to use your own feet; if you want to think or to walk, you just do it! But you do hear talk of the right to education or to a good transport system.

So rights provide access to goods and services, and are usually welcomed by the professions and others in business to provide such goods and services. If you decide to take up a right, for example to health care, you put yourself in need of a doctor. It is hardly surprising, therefore, that an American President of the late 1970s, Jimmy Carter, was keen on exporting the idea of human rights worldwide. Not only was it, for him, a genuinely moral concept, but if all human beings have a right to medical care, education, transport and the rest, then there would be markets for American capitalism for ever more.

If you really want to go the whole individualist liberal hog, then you must go along with Illich and campaign not for rights but for *liberties.* Rights to a good or service make you dependent on the producer and may be welcomed by producers; liberties enable you to do things for yourselves and are not usually welcomed by the authorities.[5] The abortion slogan is actually a liberty in this sense: a woman's liberty to choose.

The question is, do people want to go the whole hog? Are you prepared for the responsibility, and perhaps the loneliness, of being responsible only to yourself? Does hedonism — your own desires, wishes and pleasures — provide a satisfying answer to the big questions of life? Are you prepared to live with the knowledge that there is no good reason for anything other than that you desire it? Are you prepared for an existence in which nobody has any authority outside of yourself? I think there is much evidence in Part One of this book to suggest that most of us would not be at all happy with this; we want to relate not only to ourselves but also to objective reality and to the community.

Wants and desires relate only to myself. At least needs relate the self to objective reality, and open the possibility of an ethic that talks of responsibilities and obligations to our fellow human beings, and of claims upon them. The patient's needs do put an obligation upon the doctor; the child's needs do make a claim upon the mother; people's need for work does place some responsibility upon governments to do something about unemployment.

## Values

We have seen that needs ultimately derive from values. What *actually* governs people's behaviour is their values, not their needs; and social science must recognize this.[6] Also, what *should* govern people's behaviour is their values; social scientists should recognize this too and give up the fraudulent attempt to produce a moral code out of needs.

Values are ultimately held by individuals, but can be shared. They can provide a basis both for individual and communal action. People value health, so they set up some kind of health-care system. You value fidelity, so you stay by your wife. Some value the mountains, so they go climbing and will fight against despoliation.

Values provide the possibility of debate. Needs do too, but the debate is inevitably dominated by the experts, whereas there are no experts in values. Wants and desires provide the possibility of debate too, but desires have no reference point beyond the individuals who hold them and so they are a weak basis for community. Certainly one's desires may be shared by others, but generally desires are less stable than values. At the same time, it is recognized that values vary according to culture, religion and political philosophy. Values belong essentially to a community, which is exactly the level that tends to get missed out in a concept of needs that tries to relate the individual to some timeless reality.

## Abolishing Need

Though needs have formed an essential and often creative part of civilization, it will already be clear to the reader that I am very critical of the current assumption that needs should be met; rather it seems to me that we should work toward a situation in which needs do not arise in the first place. One of the few kindred spirits on this path is the late E. F. Schumacher who, in his book *Small is Beautiful,* says, 'The cultivation and expansion of needs is the antithesis of wisdom.

151

It is also the antithesis of freedom and peace . . . Only by a reduction of needs can one promote a genuine reduction in those tensions which are the ultimate causes of strife and war.'[7] Surely he is right. A third world war could well originate in the United States' need for oil, or in the Soviets' need to keep their disparate nation together, just as the Second World War originated in Germany's need for more *lebensraum.* If you need something badly enough, you'll fight for it. Certainly need provides a rationale for going to war that is more likely to carry a government's people with it than many other motives. People strive to meet their needs, and striving often leads to strife.

Schumacher looked at Buddhism for hints toward an alternative. For the Buddhist monk, it is wants that makes us unhappy; perpetual striving means perpetual frustration. The key to happiness is not to meet your wants and needs, but to reduce them, until ultimately you arrive at that state of complete emptiness that is called nirvana, 'the roaring silence'.

In my own experience, I have found that reducing wants is the key to personal contentment, but I certainly do not want a life of perpetual silent meditation. I am too much in the Western, Judaeo-Christian tradition that values activity. I firmly believe that the world, both physical and social, is not an illusion, and is worth enjoying to the full. This is the problem with the Buddhist solution, as with those early Greeks and early European socialists who exalted the man of few needs. They simply condemn us to inactivity, a life of indolence and technological backwardness. Marx was surely correct when he condemned this as 'the abstract negation of the entire world of culture and civilization, the regression to the unnatural simplicity of the poor and crude man who has few needs'.[8]

Is it possible to have a balanced society that does not set up one need after another, but is still a society in which people are motivated to work, to play, to recreate, to procreate, even though as individuals they do not need to? Is it possible for technology to be used creatively without being fuelled by needs? Is it possible to have a person of few needs who is yet not unnatural, simple, poor and crude? Is there any alternative to a needy humanistic capitalism other than a Buddhist nirvana of emptiness?

152

Schumacher knew the limitations of Buddhism. So he fused it with our own cultural heritage of Christianity and technology in his advocacy of 'intermediate technology', a technology that meets people's needs in so far as they, rather than the multinational companies, define them. Intermediate technology uses the simplest methods, the least fuel and materials that will do the job. If a bicycle will enable the Malaysian peasant to get around, there is no need to sell him a jeep. One advantage of simple technology is that it tends not to create new needs — for a continual supply of fuel, for spare parts, for replacements due to obsolescence. Schumacher hit on an approach that really does seem to keep our economic and technological needs within bounds, while at the same time allowing ample scope for innovation and creativity.

I started this book by observing that many people are very aware of the absurdity of many of our material needs, but blithely welcome the generation of need after need in other areas — marriage, childhood, employment, self-fulfilment, and so on. So too, many have latched onto Schumacher's 'small is beautiful' slogan as a way of keeping material needs within bounds, but they rarely think of applying this to their other needs, because they welcome their other needs. But if, as I have argued, our other needs are as problematic as our material needs, then can we apply Schumacher's approach to these other needs? Is there some combination of the insights of Christianity, other religions and traditions, and modern experience, that will enable us to keep these needs under control?

# 13: Liberation from Need?

I have noted how left-wing critics of corporate business attack liberals, including those of the 'New Right' variety, for their espousal of the free market. The critics show that the individual is not sovereign master over his own needs and wants, and that, far from production responding to the individual's wants, it actually creates and manipulates wants. At the same time, the Right accuse the far Left of élitism, totalitarianism and generally telling people what they really need.

So here is a paradox. Each exalts the ideal of the autonomous individual, but neither is able to provide conditions for his or her existence. How may a person be freed from being manipulated into needing? Each attacks the other in the name of liberty, but neither succeeds in showing how we may be liberated from need. *Can* we be liberated from need?

I want to suggest in this chapter that such paradoxes can be resolved only when we shed the ideal of the autonomous individual; more particularly, when we shed the ultimately anti-religious worldview of humankind as autonomous, alone in the universe, responsive to nothing but its own needs. As an alternative, I would like to draw on the Christian tradition in order to propose a view of human beings as indeed having needs and wants, some of which are valid, but none of which are looked to as the powerhouse or orientation of our lives. It was, after all, the demise of Christianity that produced the moral vacuum into which the morality of need was projected in the first place.

## Respondeo, Ergo Sum

The question is, is it possible to work, to play, to marry, to be creative, out of joyful, free, exploration of the world—or only in response to some need, either my own or someone else's?

Most philosophies since the Enlightenment have started with the individual. Descartes' famous 'Cogito, ergo sum' has this in common with Locke's 'I desire, therefore I am' and with the modern 'I need, therefore I am'. All originate in something within the individual: his or her reason, desires or needs. They all suppose a universe where there is nothing, or nothing of significance, outside of the individual.

A less lonely starting point would be 'I respond, therefore I am'. Religion would then cease to be a quest by which we seek answers to our needs for meaning and security; rather than our creating a divine being who can meet our needs, or even a pre-existing Being whose sole purpose was to meet our needs, religion would be the response of human beings to a pre-existing God.

Likewise human relationships. They would not involve human beings meeting their own needs by working, playing, loving, and so on; instead, each person would be responding to the others in his or her life. Sociology would look at how people respond to each other, rather than assume that social institutions (such as marriage) are elaborate systems for the meeting of needs. Economics would see productive activity as an opening up of the resources of the material world, rather than simply as supplying the expressed needs of the consumer.

The individual and the group would be confronted with questions: how are we to respond to God's love? How are we to respond to each other? How are we to respond to the bounteous earth? How am I to respond to my ailing body? Responding is not the same as reacting, for the person who merely reacts has little control or responsibility. Responding is the action of a responsible individual, but one who is not alone in the universe: there is something or someone to respond *to.* 'I respond, therefore I am,' makes me important, but it does not make me central and therefore does not make me lonely. Significance comes from the pre-existing what or the pre-existing who that I respond to.

The Old Testament embodies this notion of responsibility, in particular when it talks of *blessing.* God gave the Children of Israel a land flowing with milk and honey; this land is not to be struggled and striven for, but is a gift. It is different from the land of all the neighbouring countries, and certainly different from Egypt where the Israelites had been in slavery:

For the land which you are entering to take possession of it is not like the land of Egypt, from which you have come, where you sowed your seed and watered it with your feet, like a garden of vegetables;

155

but the land which you are going over to possess is a land of hills and valleys, which drinks water by the rain from heaven, a land which the Lord your God cares for; the eyes of the Lord your God are always upon it, from the beginning of the year to the end of the year.[1]

The land is not Israel's to do with as she pleases. Because it is a gift rather than the prize of battle or the profit accruing from wheeling and dealing, there are strict limits on the extent to which it can be owned. All land is to be returned to the original owner every fifty years, so that it is not possible for any one individual or family to amass large holdings.

This has similarities with the view of land held by Australian aborigines and many African tribes. The land does not belong to individuals and families. It belongs to the tribe, or to the ancestors, or is just there; everyone has rights to water and pasturage. Land is not owned by human beings after some economic, political or military struggle; it is given, by the ancestors or the spirits. It is as free as the air; nobody needs land because nobody is denied it.

There are similarities too with the modern ecological ethic. In this view, the Earth is not ours to do with as we please. Rather, it is the gift of nature, and we are to act as responsible stewards within it. Secular ecologists have realized that, if there is no God and humankind is alone within the universe, then an alternative to directing human life toward meeting human need is to direct it by responding to the universe. Human need and human greed have trampled selfishly all over the Earth. Eco-philosophy therefore is directed not to human need, but to responding respectfully to the laws of the universe and to the bounty of the Earth. This is a view of human living in response to gift. It can take either a secular form in which 'Nature' is the giver, or a more traditional religious form in which the universe is given by a creator God.

The New Testament talks of resources as gift/blessing in Jesus' parable of the talents.[2] Many a secular person sees their talents as skills or abilities which they personally possess and need to develop if they are to fulfil themselves as human beings. This is ownership plus growth: a capitalist view of the self if ever there was one! Jesus tried to get us to see our talents instead as gifts from a loving God, which we develop

156

in thanks and appreciation. For him, the purpose is not any personal need for self-fulfilment, but worship of God. Ownership is replaced by stewardship; growth by response.

The difference may be seen in men and women who are active in sports. Some are clearly striving to prove something to themselves or to others, to meet some inner need. Of these, a few have reported going off form following conversion to Christianity or another religion, because they feel their needs are now being met by their new-found faith. Personally, I find it sad that they should have been competing out of need in the first place.

Others, however, seem to play sports out of uninhibited response to their abilities and for the fun of the game. One such appears to be the West Indian cricketer Viv Richards. Watching him bat in typically irrepressible mood, it is impossible to believe other than that he shares Jesus' joyful celebration of talent.

In fact, all of us to a greater or lesser extent experience ourselves as recipients of gift as well as strivers after need. The woman who feels that she needs a child to fulfil herself, on hearing its first cry may well experience it as inexpressible gift. The ambitious man may, in a saner moment, appreciate his sheer luck in being promoted. Each time we experience ourselves as recipients of gift, then in that moment, however fleeting, we have ourselves seen the lie in all the chatter and babble about the purpose of life being no more than the challenge of meeting our own and others' needs. In that moment, which we usually call joy, we have seen beyond ourselves and our needs.


## Grace in Public

'Respondeo, ergo sum' is actually the experience of every child, though psychologists and philosophers may tell us otherwise. Generally children are born into a context of love, which pre-exists them and to which they respond and out of which they become decent human beings. Love begets love.

Millions of parents know this, yet curiously they restrict this belief in the efficacy of pre-existing love to the family. They think that if you treat people in society like that, they will abuse you. Millions in Britain are only too keen to believe that the social security system is thronged with scroungers

157

who abuse it, and many more Americans believe that a nationalized health service would erode initiative and responsibility for one's own family. People just cannot believe that you can offer love publicly without people taking advantage of you. Gratuitous, freely given, love may be the making of a child, but it is the unmaking of society. Or so people believe.

Theologians and other Christians often believe this too. They say that because of human sin, grace and love can operate only within the redeemed individual, within the Church and within that specially favoured institution, the family. The Christian message of love is applicable only to personal, church and family life; it cannot be applied to politics and economics. In this view, Christian ethics are only personal; they have no social applications, unless you count family life as 'social'. Such Christians make pronouncement after pronouncement about the family and matters related to the family, such as abortion, child-rearing, sex roles, and occasionally education, yet remain silent on virtually every other public issue. Why this utter lack of faith that grace can operate within society?

Is there in fact any evidence as to the effects one way or the other of gratuitous love shown outside the family? There is, in some quantity. In Britain there have now been over thirty years of the welfare state. Is there evidence that its policies of care have generated more care in people's hearts? Or have people responded with a 'couldn't care less attitude' that is indifferent to other people's suffering because they know someone else is paid to care? I would like to review two areas in which the evidence suggests that the welfare state *has* generated a response of compassion in ordinary people.

First, there are enormous sums of money raised in every community to buy the local hospital some new piece of equipment or the local school a swimming pool. An American friend, visiting Britain for the first time and influenced by the common American assumption that our welfare state is on the road to communism and induces dependence and apathy, was amazed to see, in a small rural town, a poster appealing for £20,000 for the local National Health Service hospital. British people believe their health and education systems to be free, and therefore more caring than a service you have to pay for. (Love after all is not love if it is paid for.) They respond by raising vast sums to support those who care for them.

An even more dramatic example, perhaps, is that Britain is virtually alone in the world in not paying any of its blood donors. In other countries, this is just not on: why, they say, would anyone give blood if there was not something in it for them? Well, in a society in which you have to pay for everything, and everybody is out for himself, this is a good question. But in Britain, as Richard Titmuss has argued persuasively,[3] the mere existence of the National Health Service has created a climate of altruism; people want to do their bit for the National Health Service, and because they get their treatment free, they wouldn't dream of wanting to be paid for donating their blood. Being cared for for free induces a response of caring for others for free.

The second area of evidence has only become available since Mrs Thatcher's government came to power in 1979. Until then, all British governments at least had made a show of caring for the poor and defenceless. What is unique about Mrs Thatcher's rhetoric is that there is no compassion in it. We must all suffer for the sake of a debatable economic theory, monetarism. The language of compassion has disappeared from official policy, and has been replaced by the dehumanized language of a technical economic theory in which there is no place for human values. Now, for all I know, the theory may be correct, but what is devastating is the disappearance of any illusion that 'they', those in power, care. If they do not care, then why should we? The British élite has always prided itself in being the moral mentor of the masses. If the élite has dehumanized public affairs, then the masses are likely to follow suit. Here surely is a major root of the riots of the summer of 1981 that amazed the world. They were the first fruit of the dehumanization, the de-caring, of public life. The authorities, too, reacted with amazement at these riots, wondering where the spirit behind them could have come from. Surely the answer is clear. The riots were the natural result of devoting the public sphere solely to technical, abstract, non-human idols. If there is no love in Westminster, why should there be any in the streets?

This apparent impermeability of the Thatcher administration to the cries of the distressed is an extreme form of its more general apparent impermeability to the wishes of the electorate. Most governments, if they find during their course of office that their policies are either not working or are becoming unpopular, will either change course or at least create the illusion of responding to public opinion. Not so Mrs Thatcher's government, which maintains the impression of steadfast loyalty to its original policies. The result is that many people now feel that the powers that be will not listen to legitimate protest, so the only way they can make themselves heard is illegitimate protest. As a result of the riots, the government did indeed appear to make a show of redressing some social evils. Implicitly, the messages coming from Mrs Thatcher are: 'Public life is an inhuman business, a matter of cold economic fact, and therefore you too may behave inhumanly,' and 'Because I will not listen to the oppressed, they will have to throw a petrol bomb to make me hear.'

I feel that this is quite strong evidence how over the past decades a modicum of grace and compassion in public life *has* generated civilized behaviour in the British people; but when these qualities appear to be absent in the leadership, then the people may well respond likewise. It is not that the masses must always follow the élite like sheep, but that love—wherever it be shown—breeds love, and callousness breeds callousness.

This is not to deny that people can and sometimes do abuse public love and concern when it is shown them, just as children often take advantage of the love shown by their parents. It could hardly be love if it were not open to abuse. But the belief that public love will inevitably and always be abused is pure ideology that will not stand up to examination. It is the ideology of the autonomous individual who must ever strive and struggle to look after himself and his own. It is the ideology of those who find it an affront that there should be anyone out there who cares.

Government in Britain since 1979 and in the United States since 1980—the Thatcher and Reagan regimes—has drawn on the philosophy of the New Right. People resented paying more taxes to pay for ever-increasing welfare services that were becoming necessary to meet ever-increasing needs; they felt that meeting need had to stop somewhere. So they voted for a government that promised to take power, and money, out of the hands of the welfare state and return it to the pockets of those who had earned it. The New Right drew on the critique of need mounted over the preceding decade by scholars of the Left who had argued that the welfare state should be made to work better, but concluded instead that the welfare state should, where possible, simply be dismantled.

This approach would return money and power to the autonomous individual, subject only to direction by a callous, inhuman, materialistic ideology. This is very different from the citizen responding to bounteous grace that I sketched earlier in this chapter. In the Thatcher/Reagan world, the person becomes isolated and naked, struggling to create their own sufficiency in a cold, harsh world where money and profit rule. In this section, I have outlined the first fruits of this approach as they have appeared in Britain in the period 1979—84. The radical Right understands the problem, our servitude to the purveyors of need, but the treatment is likely to kill the patient altogether. A society devoted to meeting human need is replaced by a society worshipping at the altar of Mammon, a 'cure' worse than the disease!

The welfare state in Britain may rightly be criticized for its monopolistic definitions of need, but even more important is its manifestation of public grace, and to lose that would be an irreparable loss. For thirty-five years, the British welfare state has been supported by traditional Conservatives and by the traditional Labour Party, both of which believed in the individual living within a caring society. This inheritance from the Christian era of the idea of pre-existing love, of pre-existing grace, is not to be lightly abandoned. It is the only thing that can redeem the secular philosophy of life as the project of meeting human need.

**Religious Implications**
The human project as the progressive meeting of human need has been unmasked; it is a secular religion, or at least a secular morality. I suggest that atheists and agnostics who pride themselves on having dispensed with morality and religion should ponder whether they have not let both in again through the back door.

Many Christians today want to leave behind a narrow

pietistic view of their religion and become more socially and politically involved. They are looking for a basis for this involvement and, not surprisingly, one of the most ready-to-hand is that they should get involved in order to meet human need.

I suggest that they should read this book, if they are not to get bogged down in all the difficulties that others who have venerated need have encountered over the past few decades. Ron Sider, for example, in his pioneering book *Rich Christians in an Age of Hunger* (1977), falls into the simple trap of dismissing socially constructed and artificial needs such as those created by advertising, and counterposing against them supposedly objective and real needs which should direct our action. He shows little awareness that all needs are socially constructed! He describes the radical redistribution of property within the early Church as follows: 'They simply gave until the needs were met. The needs of the sister and brother, not leg l property rights or future financial security, were decisive.' He gives no indication whatever of how this could be operated today in a way that even begins to surmount the difficulties I have discussed in chapters 11 and 12 of this book. I am not necessarily saying that we should abandon the concept of need, but that a little awareness of the pitfalls would not come amiss.

Until we have grappled with this, then let's stop being seduced by the spurious objectivity and apparent progressiveness of talking of our own and others' needs. Let's stick to much more honest and straightforward words: we may not be clear what our needs are, but we do know our hopes and aspirations, our loves and passions, and our fears and anxieties. Only talk of a need if you can state what it is needed *for.* And even then, be aware that there may be disagreement over whether the goal is valid, and whether there are better ways of reaching it.

Modern theology and preaching has lurched, in a hundred years, from the Victorian notion that human desires are sinful and should be restrained, to the modern notion that all human needs are good and that Jesus will meet every single one of them! There is some hope of sanity, though. The modern Anglican communion service thankfully has retained the old seventeenth-century prayer to a God who knows and understands our deepest desires and who may or may not grant them for our own good:

> Almighty God,
> to whom all hearts are open,
> all desires known,
> and from whom no secrets are hid:
> cleanse the thoughts of our hearts
> by the inspiration of your Holy Spirit,
> that we may perfectly love you,
> and worthily magnify your holy Name.[4]

The chief end of man here is the worship and enjoyment of God, not the meeting of human need. Wants, desires and needs are neither inherently good, nor inherently bad, for they have nothing to do with the purpose of life. They are means, not ends.

A loving God may or may not grant our wants and desires. But a loving God would have to meet our every need, if by need we meant the modern notion of an inherently good thing that must be met. Yet, given the absurdity of many of our modern needs, and the downright evil of some timeless needs, such as our apparent need to hate, I am sure that the last thing I want is a God who meets my every need! Then he would have become the servant of the secular society that creates most of those needs — and is that how Christians really want to see their God?

Another tendency of modern theological thinking and preaching is to link modern psychological notions of personal growth with the Christian idea of spiritual growth. Some interesting and worthwhile connections can surely be made in this respect, but one thing must be made clear. If the modern notion of personal growth is the progressive meeting of our needs, then that is not what spiritual growth is about. One supposedly basic human need is the need to be needed. One of the biggest offences of the gospel throughout the ages has been that the Christian God does *not* himself directly fulfil this need in us. We want to show God that he needs us, and so we do lots of good works and become pillars of the local church. The gospel's real offence against human pride is its claim that God does not love us because he needs our burnt offerings, but simply because of who he is. This God reveals a new way in which to live and love, not to fulfil our need to be needed but in response to being loved unconditionally. A life led in response to love, not as a search for love. A life based on abundance, not lack. A life liberated from need.

# Notes

## Chapter 1. A New Morality

1. Lest this observation appear as from yet another man pontificating on the life of women, let me say this paragraph is drawn entirely from a *woman's* study of housework: Ann Oakley, *The Sociology of Housework* (London: Martin Robertson, 1974), ch. 6.
2. See C. Wright Mills, 'Situated Actions and Vocabularies of Motive' (*American Sociological Review,* 5, 1940), pp. 904-13 and M. Scott and S. Lyman, 'Accounts' (*American Sociological Review,* 33, 1968), pp. 46—62.
3. *The German Ideology* (Moscow: Progress Publishers, 1964), p. 39.
4. Other than theism, the main alternative to finding direction to life in human needs is to find it in the universe itself. This is the alternative offered by the ecology movement. See p. 156.

## Chapter 2. The History of Need

1. For a detailed study, see Patricia Springborg, *The Problem of Human Needs and the Critique of Civilisation* (London: Allen & Unwin, 1981). Michael Ignatieff, *The Needs of Strangers* (London: Chatto and Windus, 1984) presents valuable essays on need in Shakespeare (King Lear), Augustine, Hieronymous Bosch, Erasmus, Pascal, Hume, Boswell, Adam Smith and Rousseau.
2. A. C. Macintyre in W. D. Hudson (ed.), *The Is/Ought Question* (London: Macmillan, 1969), p. 46. Also Ignatieff, ch. 3.
3. See Agnes Heller, *The Theory of Need in Marx* (London: Allison & Busby, 1976). Kate Soper, *On Human Needs* (Brighton: Harvester, 1981).
4. Ross Fitzgerald (ed.), *Human Needs and Politics* (Sydney: Pergamon, 1977), p. ix.

## Chapter 3. Material Needs

1. J. A. Walter, 'Family Car' (*Town & Country Planning,* 50, (2), Feb. 1981), pp. 56—9.
2. On the moral ambiguity of loving wife and family at the expense of others, see C. S. Lewis, *The Four Loves* (London: Fontana, 1963); also Ferdinand Mount, *The Subversive Family* (London: Cape, 1982).

3. Quoted by T. H. Marshall, 'The Philosophy and History of Need', in R. W. Canvin and N. G. Pearson, *Needs of the Elderly* (University of Exeter, 1973).

4. *Economic and Philosophical Manuscripts of 1844* (London: Lawrence & Wishart, 1970), p. 147.

5. A notable exception is Mary Douglas and Baron Isherwood, *The World of Goods* (New York: Basic Books, 1978).

6. Vance Packard, *The Hidden Persuaders* (Harmondsworth: Penguin, 1960); J. K. Galbraith, *The Affluent Society* (Harmondsworth: Pelican 1962).

7. An exception is G. Becker, *The Economic Approach to Human Behaviour* (University of Chicago Press 1976). Ray Pahl's *Division of Labour* (Oxford: Blackwell, 1984) is an important sociological study of the informal economy.

8. K. Marx, *The Poverty of Philosophy* (London: Lawrence & Wishart, 1955), p. 29.

9. Roger Miller, *Economics Today* (San Francisco: Canfield Press, 1973), p. 38.

10. M. Sahlins, *Stone Age Economics* (Chicago: Aldine, 1972).

11. For example, D. P. Ghai *et al, The Basic Needs Approach to Development* (Geneva: International Labour Office, 1977).

12. William Leiss, *The Limits to Satisfaction* (London: Marion Boyars, 1978), p. 39. Some of the other quotes in this section are also drawn from Leiss. Not all environmentalists hold this view of plenty; some consider resources to be distinctly finite, and they castigate multi-national companies for assuming that new resources will always be found.

13. Tibor Scitovsky, *The Joyless Economy* (Oxford University Press, 1976).

14. Richard Lipsey, *Economics* (New York: Harper & Row, 1973, 4th edn), p. 5.

**Chapter 4. The Needs of the Self**

1. Romans 7.21—5 (RSV).

2. Daniel Yankelovich, 'New Rules in American Life' (*Psychology Today,* April 1981), p. 40.

3. Abraham Maslow, *Toward a Psychology of Being* (New York: Van Nostrand, 2nd edn 1968), p. 35.

4. Abraham Maslow, *Motivation and Personality* (New York: Harper & Row, 2nd edn 1970), p. xxii.

5. ibid, p. 266.

6. Yankelovich, op. cit., p. 40.

7. C. Disbrey, 'A Question of Behaviour' (*Third Way,* Feb. 1983), pp. 13—15.

8. See P. Vitz, *Psychology as Religion* (Tring: Lion, 1979).
9. Victor Frankl, *Man's Search for Meaning* (London: Hodder, 1964), pp. 112—3.
10. E. Fromm, 'The Psychology of Normalcy' (*Dissent,* vol.1, 1954), p. 43.
11. H. Marcuse, *One Dimensional Man* (London: Routledge, 1964), p. 6.

## Chapter 5. Need in Work and Leisure

1. Robert Marshall, 'The Problem of the Wilderness' (*Scientific Monthly,* Feb. 1930), p. 143.
2. D. Revelle, 'Outdoor Recreation in a Hyper-Productive Society' (*Daedalus,* 96, 1967), p. 1174.
3. Kenneth Roberts *et al,* 'Youth Unemployment: an old problem or a new life style?' (*Leisure Studies,* 1 (2), May 1982), pp. 171—82.
4. See Tony Walter, *Hope on the Dole* (London: SPCK, 1985).
5. *Radio Times,* 7 Sept. 1982.

## Chapter 6. The Needs of the Sexes

1. S. Hite, *The Hite Report on Male Sexuality* (Macdonald, 1981).
2. 'Shere Hite on Maleness and Mixed Feelings' (*Spare Rib,* 112, Nov. 1981), pp. 18—21.
3. Christopher Lasch, *Haven in a Heartless World* (New York: Basic Books, 1977), p. 197.
4. M. Young and P. Willmott, *Family and Kinship in East London* (London: Routledge, 1957).
5. 'Shere Hite on Maleness', op.cit., p. 19.
6. Willard Waller, 'The Rating and Dating Complex' (*American Sociological Review,* 2, 1937).
7. C. S. Lewis, op.cit., p. 88.

## Chapter 7. Children's Needs

1. Ann Dally, *Inventing Motherhood* (London: Burnett/Hutchinson, 1982), ch. 5.
2. Alan Storkey, *A Christian Social Perspective* (Leicester: Inter Varsity Press, 1979). p. 231.
3. B. Spock, *Baby and Child Care* (New English Library, 1969), p. 24.

4. M. K. Pringle, *The Needs of Children* (London: Hutchinson, 1974), pp. 148, 161.
5. U. Bronfenbrenner, *Two Worlds of Childhood* (London, Allen & Unwin, 1971); the quote is from pp. 8 – 9.
6. On the family as a universe, see Peter Berger and Hansfried Kellner, 'Marriage and the Construction of Reality' (*Diogenes*, 46, 1964), pp. 1 – 25.
7. Quoted in Lasch, *Haven in a Heartless World*, p. 74.
8. Anthony Flew, 'Wants or Needs, Choices or Commands', in Fitzgerald, op. cit. Also see R. F. Dearden, 'Needs in Education', in R. F. Dearden *et al, Education and the Development of Reason* (London: Routledge, 1972), pp. 50 – 64.
9. Anthony Flew, 'Philosophising About Education' (*New Humanist*, 88, April 1973), pp. 482 – 3.

## Chapter 8. Welfare Needs

1. G. Smith, *Social Need* (London: Routledge, 1980).
2. Ian Sinclair, 'Personal Needs and Moral Dilemmas', in Noel Timms, *Social Welfare* (London: Routledge, 1980).
3. See Timms, op. cit., and Raymond Plant *et al.* (eds.), *Political Philosophy and Social Welfare* (London: Routledge, 1980) for recent British contributions to the philosophy of welfare.
4. Sinclair, op. cit., pp. 282-3.
5. From 'XII The Human Abstract', in *Songs of Experience* by William Blake.
6. J. A. Walter, 'The Scene of the Crime' (*Third Way*, Nov. 1978), pp. 16 – 17, and 'Toward Eliminating the Jericho Road' (*Howard Journal*, 19 (1), 1980), pp. 17 – 26.
7. J. Bradshaw, 'The Concept of Social Need' (*New Society*, 30 March 1972, pp. 640 – 3), effectively argues along these lines.

## Chapter 9. Explaining Need

1. P. Springborg, *The Problem of Human Needs and the Critique of Civilisation*, p. 151.
2. Alasdair Macintyre, *Marcuse* (London: Fontana, 1970), p. 72.
3. Leiss, op. cit.
4. Springborg, op. cit., p. 153.
5. Maslow *is* explicit about this.

## Chapter 10. Needs Must

1. Robin Horton, 'African Traditional Thought and Western Science' (*Africa*, 37, 1967).

2. See Springborg, op. cit., appendix; also Paul Taylor, 'Need Statements' (*Analysis,* 19), pp. 106—11.

## Chapter 11. The Price of Need

1. Sprinbgborg, op. cit., p. 152.
2. Maslow, *Motivation and Personality.*
3. ibid, p. xv.
4. Christopher Lasch, *The Culture of Narcissism* (New York: W. W. Norton, 1978), p. 27.
5. Ivan Illich, *Disabling Professions* (London: Marion Boyars, 1977), pp. 14—15.
6. J. Jacobs, *The Death and Life of Great American Cities* (New York: Random House, 1961).
7. Yankelovich, op. cit., p. 50.

## Chapter 12. Alternatives to Need

1. F. A. Hayek, *Studies in Philosophy, Politics and Economics* (London: Routledge, 1967).
2. Leiss, op. cit., pp. 72—3.
3. Plant *et al.,* op. cit.
4. Bradshaw, op. cit.
5. Ivan Illich, *Toward a History of Need* (New York: Pantheon, 1977), p. 43.
6. As anthropologist Dorothy Lee argued persuasively back in 1948. See her article 'Are Basic Needs Ultimate?' in D. D. Lee, *Freedom and Culture* (Englewood Cliffs: Prentice Hall, 1959), pp. 70—7.
7. E. F. Schumacher, *Small is Beautiful* (London: Abacus, 1974), p. 26.
8. K. Marx, *Collected Works,* vol.3 (London: Lawrence & Wishart, 1975).

## Chapter 13. Liberation from Need?

1. Deuteronomy 11. 10—12 (RSV). See Walter Brueggemann, *The Land* (Philadelphia: Fortress Press, 1977).
2. Matthew 25. 14—30.
3. R. Titmuss, *The Gift Relationship,* (Harmondsworth: Penguin, 1970).
4. The Collect of Purity from the Order for Holy Communion Rite A in the Alternative Service Book 1980.

# Index

170